D0472979

COMMUNICATION

AND

INTERPERSONAL RELATIONSHIPS

_____

How To Say What You Mean To Say

Dave Marks

National Writing Institute
Denton, Texas

Copyright © 1996 - 2004 by Dave Marks

All rights reserved. No part of this book may be used or reproduced in any manner whatsoever without written permission except in the case of brief quotations embodied in critical articles and reviews.

ISBN: 1-888344-15-6

Printed in the United States of America.

For information write: National Writing Institute,
                           624 W. University # 248
                           Denton TX 76201

or call: (800) 688-5375

National Writing Institute website address: www.writingstrands.com

NATIONAL WRITING INSTITUTE PUBLICATIONS

STUDENTS

Writing Strands Level 1
Writing Strands Level 2
Writing Strands Level 3
Writing Strands Level 4
Writing Strands Level 5
Writing Strands Level 6
Writing Strands Level 7
Writing Exposition
Creating Fiction
Communication and Interpersonal Relationships
Dragonslaying is For Dreamers
Axel Meets the Blue Men
Axel's Challenge

_____

PARENTS/TEACHERS

Evaluating Writing
Reading Strands
Analyzing the Novel:
Dragonslaying is for Dreamers
Lessons From Fiction:
Axel Meets the Blue Men

PREFACE

This is a book about the uses and effects of your communication techniques in your relationships with people who are close to you. Words are so important a part of what we do, what we think and what creates the bonds between us, that our lives truly are controlled and defined by them. How we use words and to what purposes we use them, determines the types of people we are.

Most of us cannot go for twenty-four hours without saying something unkind about another person. If you doubt this, keep a listing of what you say and hear in a one-day period that would hurt those talked about. I think you'll be surprised at how often hurt-filled words are spoken by most people who don't realize what they're doing.

There probably is no part of life in which so many of us violate the Golden Rule. One reason is that we were brought up to think that "Sticks and stones can break my bones but words can never hurt me." As much as this sounds nice and even rhymes, it's just not true. Words can lead to pain and hatred as well as to love. We should be constantly aware of how they are used.

It may be hard to understand the justice of it, but we are, in other people's eyes, what they have heard about us. We are defined by the words of others, just as we create the feelings about people when we talk about them.

Your ability to use words to effect your desires can be a tremendous asset to you. The techniques presented in this book should enable you to use your words to develop thoughtful interactions with those who are close to you and to keep those relationships positive.

CONTENTS
page

USING THIS BOOK

This is not a speech course, or even a book about making speeches. There are lots of those and some are very good. If you want to learn to make public speeches, your library should have many fine aids.

These exercises will help you relate to others in ways that will allow you to understand what you both are feeling and saying. They were designed for teenagers. If there are some that you don't understand, that's fine; wait for a year or so and try them again.

You can practice all of these techniques this year and practice them again a couple years from now and then again later and gain more understanding and skill each time around.

This is not a textbook to be used in a school. Most of the techniques presented are too complicated for classroom use. The exercises are best practiced at home. Many of the skills offered here are ones that most parents would like their children to have exposure to.

I taught in public schools for 30 years, and I never heard of these kinds of skills being taught in classrooms. And yet, they are so very important for young people to have, or have a chance to learn.

If you have bought this book for yourself or for your family, you should have the people using it read through an exercise together, discuss the ideas, and work out the strategies for doing them. It's not necessary to keep any regular schedule. What is important is that young people learn to communicate with others in ways that will produce pleasant and productive relationships.

EYE CONTACT

This exercise will help you to understand:
1. The conventions of eye contact in conversations for:
    A. Speakers

    B. Listeners
2. The security in conversations where the conventions are kept
3. The insecurity in conversations where the conventions are broken

UNDERSTANDINGS

One of the conventions (the way we do things) of conversation in our culture is that the listener looks at the speaker's eyes or face about 80% of the time the speaker is talking. The speaker looks at the listener's eyes/face only about 15 to 20% of the time. These percentages aren't true unless the two people feel that they're equal. That is, if they're about the same age or if they feel equal in social position.

For example, if an adult is talking to a child, the adult looks at the child's eyes/face more than that percentage of the time. This proves especially true if the adult's in the act of teaching, scolding or correcting the child. In these cases the percentages are almost reversed.

This exercise is designed to give you an understanding of this convention and to give you an experience with its violation. You'll understand the effects of this violation on your interactions as you perceive your conversational partners beginning to realize that something is wrong or unusual about the conversations you're having.

EXERCISE

There are two parts to this exercise:

PART ONE

You're to have three conversations and take notes about the eye/face contacts of both you and the person you're talking with. These notes should be about both when you're speaking and when you're listening to your conversational partners.

Of course, you're not to tell your partners what you're studying so as to avoid influencing the outcome. You'll be having conversations with three people for this part of the exercise.

1. The first conversation will be with someone your own age.
2. The second will be with an adult, other than your parents.
3. The third will be with an adult—again not one of your parents—and you'll be asking for information or directions about how to get somewhere or to do something.

Your notes for these conversations might look like the following examples:

FIRST CONVERSATION

WHEN I WAS SPEAKING TO A FRIEND MY AGE:

M (me):   Talked about my trip to the (store, beach, or whatever). I started the conversation with e/c (eye contact) about 20% of the time. This seemed to be a normal conversation and my friend's reactions were what I expected them to be after reading about eye contact.

F (friend): As he listened to me, he had the normal amount of e/c. It was about 80-90% of the time.

WHEN MY FRIEND WAS SPEAKING:

M: I kept e/c while he was speaking to me about 80% of the time. I could see that he felt at ease with me and the conversation.

When you've finished with the three conversations and have made the notes, you'll have a good understanding about the nature of the convention of conversational eye contact for people in our culture.

Other cultures have different conventions. In some cultures, both parties give almost total eye contact. In others it is an insult for one person to look directly into the eyes of another while conversing.

PART TWO

You're now to violate the conventions of eye contact and to record the reactions of your conversation partners.

You're to pick the same people or people who are like the ones in the first conversations and have similar conversations with them. This means that you'll have three more conversations:

1. This time when you're speaking, you're to look, most of the time, directly into the eyes of the people you're speaking with while you're talking.
2. You should look away most of the time the other people are speaking.

Take notes about your partners' reactions to these violations of the conventions of eye contact. Watch for any indications of your partners becoming nervous. You can tell this by their beginning to fidget with things, look around the room, tap their fingers or blink rapidly.

This experience should give you some new understandings about your conversations and make it possible to demonstrate respect for the ideas of the people with whom you talk. When you're done with these exercises, you'll understand much more about what's of interest to people when you talk with them.

Keep in mind that it's not a kind thing to intentionally make other people uncomfortable or nervous, and it might make them less than eager to talk with you in the future. If you feel you've made someone uncomfortable with this exercise, it might be wise, after the conversation, to explain what you've been studying.

VERBAL REINFORCEMENT

This exercise will help you to understand:

1. How people reinforce others in conversation
2. How this understanding can benefit you in your conversations

UNDERSTANDINGS

We all reinforce the speaker when we're in conversations. To reinforce what someone has said is to encourage that person to go on talking. This isn't something we were taught directly by our parents or friends. It's something we learned to do when we were four or five years old by watching how other people acted when they had conversations.

Reinforcing someone or something someone has said is a way to say to that person *I understand what you're saying*, or, *What you're saying is interesting to me,* or, *I agree with you.*

We each have our own methods of reinforcement and they're different for different situations. We learned what worked best for us as we practiced having conversations after watching how the adults in our families used reinforcements when they were talking together.

Even though we all have special ways to reinforce our conversational partners, there are some general rules for this. Most people reinforce what others say by:
1. Saying *Yeah* or *Yes*, *Go on* or *Sure* or *Okay* or *Uh huh*, or *Cool*, or *Right on*
2. Grunting
3. Repeating what was just said
4. Smiling or laughing

Another part of this convention of reinforcement is when the speaker asks for reinforcement. We're so used to this happening in our conversations that we're not conscious of being asked to reinforce what is being said to us. As you have the four conversations in this exercise, watch for how people ask you to reinforce what they've said. They will:

1. Raise the pitch of their voices almost as if asking questions.

> *"You go two blocks down and turn left. You'll see a McDonald's on the corner. Turn there. . . At the McDonald's?"*

4

You'll find that the speaker will raise his voice on the last sentence. He'll be asking you if you understand where you're to turn left. If you reinforce what he's just said in some manner, he'll go on and tell you the rest of the directions. If you don't reinforce him, he'll most likely go over again the same directions. He'll feel you don't understand where to turn. This works the same way even when one person isn't asking directions; when people are just talking together.

2. Raise their eyebrows.
   This acts in the same way as raising the voice does. It's a request for the listener to acknowledge that the speech is understood.
3. Pause and look at the listener.
   If this doesn't work, the speakers try other request-for-reinforcement methods.
4. Raise both hands and spread them outward, and at the same time nod the head and lift the eyebrows. This is a very strong request for reinforcement and isn't common for ordinary conversations. It's used by people in authority when explaining something to younger people who don't understand what to do or to employees who have done something wrong.
5. Pause and look the listeners in the eye. If this doesn't get a reinforcement, then the speakers make a sound almost like clearing the throat or humming and again look at the listeners.

EXERCISES

There are two parts to this exercise:

In the first part you'll have two conversations:

1. You're to have two conversations in which you reinforce in the normal ways what the speakers say; and
2. You're to have two conversations in which you don't reinforce what the speakers say.

PART ONE

In the first set of conversations, you're to have one where you ask for directions to a well known place, and you're to give normal reinforcements. The other conversation can be about anything your partner wants to talk about and you're to again reinforce the speaker.

PART TWO

In the second two conversations, you're to have one where you ask for directions, but you'll not reinforce anything the speaker says. You'll find that this is hard to do. You've become so accustomed to the conventions of reinforcement that you'll have to concentrate to be able to avoid reinforcing the speaker.

When I was learning about these reinforcement conventions, I did these things I'm suggesting you do. I remember asking directions of a gas station attendant who was out by the pumps.

I didn't reinforce what he told me, and after repeating the directions a number of times, he asked me to get out of the car and come to the curb with him. He took me to the edge of the road and pointed in the direction I was to go. He then pointed out the place where I was to turn. I was careful not to let on that I had understood this all along. He would have been embarrassed.

The second conversation will be about anything your partner wants to talk about. You'll again have to concentrate so that you don't reinforce your speaking partner.

You should take notes about these two sets of conversations. They might be similar to the notes that you took for the "Eye Contact" exercise. In your notes for the conversations where you reinforce what the speaker says, you should record three things:
1. What types of reinforcements you used
2. How often you used reinforcements
3. Your speaker's reactions to your reinforcements

In your notes for the conversations where you don't reinforce what the speaker says, you should record:
1. The speaker's reactions when you didn't reinforce what was said
2. What devices the speaker used to get you to reinforce what was being told to you

You'll find that when you don't reinforce the speech of the people you're with, they get nervous. They feel you don't understand what they're saying or that you don't agree with them.

If you're successful in not reinforcing the speech of the people talking to you, they'll continually ask for reinforcement. I have a friend who, when I don't reinforce what she says, reaches out and touches my arm. Sometimes she even grabs the arms of people she is talking with so as to get more reinforcement.

PHYSICAL REINFORCEMENT

This exercise will help you to understand:

1. The common physical methods of reinforcement
2. The effectiveness of physical reinforcement on speakers' attitudes
3. The effect of negative physical reactions and non-reinforcements on speakers' attitudes

UNDERSTANDINGS

The conventions of physical reinforcement are as well known and as widely used as the verbal ones. We let our conversational partners know we do or don't understand what they're saying and how we feel about what they're saying by the ways we react with our bodies to what is being said. We do this by:
1. Nodding
2. Smiling
3. Glancing at the eyes of the speakers
4. Leaning forward or toward the speakers
5. Opening up body posture (turning toward the speakers)

We also indicate to speakers that we don't agree with them or don't understand what they're saying by giving negative body reinforcements. We do this by:
1. Downturning or flattening the lips
2. Shaking the head
3. Turning the face away
4. Casting the eyes upward and/or sighing
5. Turning the shoulders away from the speaker
6. Crossing the arms over the chest
7. Crossing the legs away from the speaker
8. Showing obvious interest in something else, such as a piece of lint on clothing or what other people are doing

EXERCISES

You're to have four conversations in the two parts of this exercise:

1. You're to have **two** conversations (not asking directions):
   A. One in which you reinforce **just with your body** what the speaker says

B. One in which you reinforce **both with your voice and your body** what the speaker says

2. You're to have two other conversations:

A. One in which you **don't reinforce** in any way what the speaker says
B. One in which you **give negative reinforcements** (both voice and body) to what is said to you

PART ONE

These two conversations will be harder for you to engineer because you'll be with people who'll want to talk to you. In these instances, you'll be indicating to these people that you don't want to talk to them or that you don't understand what they're saying or that you don't agree with them.

To make this a meaningful experience, you'll have to find people who want to talk to you, and you might have to try a few times before you're successful. That's okay, because the benefit you'll get from really understanding the power you'll have with your command of positive and negative reinforcements will make the effort worthwhile.

1. The first conversation will be hard because you'll have to reinforce with *only your body* and control your verbal reinforcements. You might have to try this conversation a few times before you're successful. It's hard to give just body reinforcements. You'll find that you'll have to concentrate very hard to keep from giving verbal indications of how you feel.
2. The second conversation will be with you *reinforcing with both your voice and your body* what the speaker says to you. You'll be surprised at how easily you'll be able to understand how the speaker feels about talking with you.

PART TWO

In these two conversations you're to indicate to the speakers by *negative body and voice non-reinforcements* that you're not interested in the conversations you're having.

You'll find that the speakers will quickly lose interest in talking with you. They might even become upset with your showing a lack of interest in what they have to say. When you notice this, it will be time to stop the conversations and explain what you're doing.

Be very careful with this understanding of how other people feel. Keep in mind that with any knowledge comes responsibility. If you find that you understand how other people feel, you have the responsibility not to make them feel badly about themselves.

When done, it might be a good idea to talk with them about what you were doing when you were talking with them. You might explain that you were doing an exercise in reinforcements so that they don't feel embarrassed.

1. In this second set of conversations, you're to have one where you ask for directions, but you'll not reinforce anything the speaker says. You'll find that this is hard to do. You've become so accustomed to the conventions of reinforcement that you'll have to concentrate to be able to avoid reinforcing the speaker.
2. The second conversation will be about anything the speaker wants to talk about. You'll again have to concentrate so that you don't reinforce your speaking partner, but even more, this time you're to give your partner negative reinforcements. Negative reinforcements are just the opposite of positive reinforcements. Do the opposite of what you did to positively reinforce. For instance, you nodded your head to reinforce what was just said to you. To negatively reinforce, you would shake your head. Instead of looking into the eyes of the speaker, look around the room or look at something in your hands.

You should take notes about these two sets of conversations. They might be similar to the notes that you took for the "Eye Contact" exercise.

In your notes for the conversations where you reinforce what the speaker said, you should record three things:

1. What types of reinforcements you used
2. How often you used reinforcements
3. Your speaker's reactions to your reinforcements

In your notes for the conversations where you didn't reinforce what the speaker said and even gave negative reinforcements, you should record:

1. The speaker's reactions when you didn't reinforce what was said
2. What devices the speaker used to get you to reinforce what was being told to you when you used negative reinforcements

Remember that if speakers don't get reinforcements or if they get negative reinforcements for what they say, they'll often do things to get the reinforcements they need to feel comfortable. They will:

1. Repeat what they have just said
2. Talk louder
3. Reach out and touch their listeners
4. Raise their eyebrows
5. Nod
6. Even ask if they're understood

Remember that when you don't reinforce the speech of the people you're with, they get nervous. They feel that you don't understand what they're saying or that you don't agree with them. Again, keep in mind that it isn't kind to make people feel uncomfortable. If you find that you've done this, you might explain what you've been studying.

MEETING PEOPLE

Those things that your parents told you about first impressions being important are true. You'll have just one chance in your life to meet anyone for the first time. What your body and voice tell that person about you during this encounter will stay with that person for a long time. It's possible to change another's first impression of you, but, to do this, you have to be very conscious of what that impression was in the first place and what parts of it you want to change. You then must plan on how you're going to change that person's mind about you and then take the time to do it. As you can see, it makes more sense to make the impression you desire on the first meeting.

UNDERSTANDINGS

There are a number of ways you have of demonstrating to others during this first meeting just what kind of a person you are. You'll be telling about yourself and how you feel about meeting that other person by the way you:

1. Shake hands
2. Look at the person
3. Choose the first words you say
4. Stand
5. Let your face talk

Of course, the actions in this list will depend on:

1. Your age
2. The age of the person you're meeting
3. The circumstances of the meeting

This can get complicated, but generally the circumstances will break down similar to this:

1. Your age:
   A. 10 or under
   B. 11-15
   C. 16-20
2. The age of the person you're meeting:
   A. Same age as you
   B. You're older (by 4 - 10 years)
   C. You're younger (by 10 - 20 years)

3. The situation of the meeting
    A. Formal (new boss, teacher, minister, group leader)
    B. Informal (new member of group, neighbor, friend of a friend, teammate)

The way you feel about the meeting and your prior training will dictate to you your attitude in any meeting in any of the above situations. But, it's important to understand that there are some general rules about meeting people under any circumstance. It's best to do two things on first meetings:

1. Show respect
2. Indicate that you enjoy the opportunity of meeting that person

Let's go back to the first list—how you tell about yourself.

1. Shaking Hands

Shaking hands is a gesture of friendship and an offering to be non-aggressive. You want to say to the other person, regardless of age, that you're a positive and friendly person. To do this you'll have to do the following:

A. Look other people in the eye as you shake hands. You'll have a tendency to want to look at the two hands to make sure you won't miss the other person's hand. This isn't necessary. You'll never miss. Practice this with your parents or your brothers or sisters. You'll find that you'll be able to look other people in the eye and still know where their hands are. This is especially important when shaking the hands of people who are older than you are. This says about you that you have a great deal of confidence in your meeting with them.

Notice that, when you shake hands with people your age or ones who are younger than you are, they look at your hand to make sure that they don't miss it. To do this you'll have to watch their eyes. This will be good practice for looking into the eyes of others when you shake their hands.

B. Give a firm, but not hard, hand clasp. This will take practice. If the person you're shaking the hand of is younger than you are, be gentle. It is easy to hurt other smaller hands, and this won't say about you what you want said. If you're under 15 years old, let the older person initiate (offer) the hand shaking.

If the person is your age or younger, you've the choice of whether to shake hands or not. If the other person offers, of course, you'll respond by offering your hand. Otherwise be guided by how you feel about the meeting.

If you're shaking the hand of a person who is older, let that person do the arm pumping. You just hang on and follow along. Remember, look into the eyes.

If you're a male, always allow a girl or woman to initiate the hand shaking. Never start this ritual yourself.

Be firm, but not hard with the hand. If you're a girl, these last few rules are reversed for you. Practice with your father or brothers. If you're about 15, you can initiate this ritual as you see fit.

C. Don't pump your arm when you shake hands. You'll run into people who'll pump your arm like it's an old-fashioned water pump and they're trying to get water to flow out of your mouth. Resist doing this yourself. One or two slight pumps is fine, but remember, *slight*.

2. Looking at the Person

When we look at people's eyes and at their faces when we meet them, we're saying to them: *I like what I see*. Do this. It's important. If you're like the rest of us in this respect, you'll have a tendency to look away from the faces of the people you meet after first establishing eye contact. It'll take some practice to get over this. Work on it. It'll pay big dividends (rewards). Later in the "exercise" portion of this activity, you should design one exercise to practice this very important skill.

3. The First Words You Say

"It's nice to meet you," is always good. This, accompanied by looking into the eyes and smiling as you offer to shake hands, will go a long way in saying what you feel about the meeting.

It's especially important to use the other person's name when you meet for the first time. We all like to hear our names spoken. This says that you heard the name in the introduction, cared enough to remember it, and that you think the name is important. Try this with an older person while shaking hands and smiling: "It's nice to meet you, Mr Jones."

With a person younger than you are, you might say something similar to: "It's nice to meet you, Billy," and immediately follow it with, "Where do you go to school?" or, "How long have you been homeschooling?" or "Did you like the meeting today?" This will give the younger person something to talk about and will make the meeting less tense. Notice how much more comfortable you feel meeting older people when they give you an opening to speak in this way.

You should practice using the names of people you've just met in the conversations that follow the meetings. This will greatly impress the people you're talking with and will help you remember their names so that the next time you see them you'll be able to use their names. There might be a conversation similar to the following one where you're meeting a person we'll call Mr. Jones. Notice how your use of Mr. Jones' name sounds comfortable. And it will be comfortable for you to do this with just a little practice:

"How do you do, Mr. Jones? It's nice to meet you."

"Hi, Bill. Your dad has said some wonderful things about the skills you're picking up in your homeschooling."

"Thanks, that's good to hear, Mr. Jones. Learning at home's a great opportunity for me. I like it lots better than when I was in school in town."

"How long have you been doing this, Bill?"

"Three years now. Oh, there's my little sister. I've got to catch her to take her home with me. It was good talking to you, Mr. Jones."

This very short conversation should illustrate for you the friendliness and warmth shown by using other people's names when you talk to them.

After you've talked with people you've just met, you'll have another opportunity to let them know that you've enjoyed meeting them. You can again smile, use their names and tell them that you enjoyed meeting them. You might try: "It was nice meeting you, Mr. Jones," as you smile and extend your hand.

This will also take some practice. Don't be embarrassed to practice this with your family. All older people had to learn these techniques, and your parents will appreciate that you're learning to do these things.

4. How You Stand

It will help you understand that your stance talks about the kind of person you are and how you feel about the meeting if you watch the way other people stand when they're meeting and talking together.

I would think that you'd want to be seen as a person who feels good about the meeting and who has a good self-image. This means that, by the way you stand, you're saying two things to the person you're meeting:

A. I'm interested, eager, and glad that I'm meeting you; and,

B. I like myself and I'm ready to like you.

14

You can say these things if you stand erectly. This sounds like Mom saying "Stand up straight," and it is. But it's important because of what it says about you.

You might want to practice stepping forward one short step as you offer your hand. This lets the other person know that you've confidence in the meeting and in yourself. If you hang back and let the other person step forward to meet you, you're saying just the opposite.

C. Lean forward a bit when you offer your hand. If you don't do this, the other person will have to lean forward for both of you, and this might give the message that you're not eager to make contact with him or her.

5. How You Talk With Your Face

There's nothing you can do that will be more important in saying that you enjoy meeting someone than in showing your teeth. Smile! This may sound dumb and phony, but it's not and it's a very powerful message about how you feel. We all like to be liked. We like to feel that other people approve of us. A smile does this. It says: "I like what I see and I like meeting you."

A good place to observe these patterns of behavior as people meet is just before and after church. People often shake hands then as they greet each other. Your minister will be shaking hands with many people after the service. Watch what he does in relationship to the five points listed at the start of this exercise:

A. Watch how he holds his hand when he's offering it to others. Notice how differently he shakes the hands of the women.

B. Watch very carefully the way he uses his eyes when he greets people. Does he look at their eyes, or lips, or both, and when does he do this?

C. Note what he says to people. Does he speak differently to people he has just met than he does to people he's known for some time? What's the difference? You'll find that he uses people's names as he greets them.

D. Make notes of the different ways people stand when they meet. Make notes about what you felt they were saying about themselves by the ways they used their bodies.

E. Notice the smiles. Do they smile only when they're greeting or do the smiles carry over into their conversations? What do you think the difference is in how the people feel about their meetings?

EXERCISE

In order for you to learn this skill, you'll have to practice meeting people a good number of times. Since I can't plan these meetings for you, you'll have to design the exercises to practice these principles.

You might ask your family to help you practice and then ask each member to introduce you to people. You could even ask them to notice how well you do on each of the points you're practicing. You could keep notes on how well you do and what the reactions are of the other people. This will tell you how much practice you still need.

If you ask your parents or friends to introduce you to people they know but you don't know, so that you might practice, they'll be happy to help you. Don't be discouraged if the first few meetings feel awkward. The more times you practice meeting people, the better you'll get at it.

CLASSROOM TECHNIQUES

The chances are now that you're working with these communication techniques at home, but soon you may be in a classroom with others, and it's going to be much different. Many students who study at home go to public or church schools for their junior or senior high school classes. In some towns, kids can go to public school for those classes that are very hard to take at home. These might include advanced math, science, or foreign language. So, you very well might be in a classroom situation even before you go to college (if that's what you've planned).

UNDERSTANDINGS

It's very rare for students in public school to have had any training in how to talk in an academic setting. Most kids learn how to deal with their verbal educational needs by trial and error. This works for some, but not very well for most.

In groups like those found in classrooms, you won't have an opportunity to work with people who love and understand you the way your family does. In groups of other students, you'll have to be much more responsible for what you say and how you say it. You can best meet these needs by learning to:

1. Ask questions
2. Answer questions
3. Request more information on points you don't understand
4. Present views or ideas that are in conflict with what others have said
5. Defend your ideas and opinions
6. Be effective while talking to a group

EXERCISES

It would be very hard for you to do exercises in these skills with classroom-size groups of people, so you'll have to work with small groups of friends or with members of your family. They should be willing to help you develop these skills.

ASKING QUESTIONS I

Most kids don't understand how to ask questions of their teachers in classrooms because they aren't given exercises that teach them to do so. This isn't a hard skill to learn, but it will take some thought on your part.

The thing you'll have to keep in mind is that when you ask a question in a room full of people, you're taking time away from everyone in the room. Every one of them has to wait for you to ask your question and then wait through the answer. You'll have to learn to use their time carefully. If you go to college, you'll be taking the time of other students who also paid lots of money to be there, and everyone in the class will appreciate you being precise in your questions.

One of the main problems with asking for information is that you'll have to ask questions in such a way that the answers you're given are the ones you really want.

What usually happens in classes, and even at home with parents, is that the adult answering the question has to figure out what the person asking really wants to know and then give that information. Often in classes, students don't ask the questions that will give them the answers they seek. There's a good deal of interpretation necessary for a teacher to be able to understand what information is desired and then give it.

An example of a typical question of this type is when a teacher says, Do all the problems on page 19. The question might be, *Do you mean all the problems on the whole page?*

The student doesn't want to know what problems to do. He was just told that. What he wants to do is say that he thinks there are too many problems on that page and he doesn't want to do so many. He wants reassurance that he'll be able to do the assignment without too much work for one night.

The teacher in this case would not say, *Yes, all the problems*. She would know what the student really wanted and so she'd answer this way: *The problems are very small and simple. We've practiced them in class, and you'll be able to do the page in a very short time.*

The student will have gotten what he needed but not what he asked for. What he should have said, if he really had wanted to ask the question he wanted the answer to, would have been: *I feel there may be too many problems on that page for us to do in just one night. Why do you feel that it is reasonable to ask us to do them all?*

It will help you to understand how common this problem is if you go to drug, grocery, fast food or convenience stores and ask clerks for something. You'll find that the conversations will be similar to these on the next page:

> *"Where are the aspirins?"*
> *"Aspirins?"*
> *"Yes, where are the aspirins?"*
> *"Aisle six."*

or,

"I would like a small Coke with lemon."
"A small Coke with lemon?"
"Yes, a small Coke with lemon."
"With lemon, right?"

Clerks almost always repeat the names of the items asked for. I don't understand why, but they do. They don't want the answers the questions they ask require. They know the answers, or they couldn't repeat the name of the desired items.

When you want information in a classroom situation, you'll have to decide:

1. Exactly what you need to know; not generally, but precisely what you want
2. In what form you want the answer: a yes or no, an explanation, a justification (reasons) for a position, arguments that support a view, or further discussion of a general nature on the subject at hand
3. Exactly how to phrase the question to get what you want (In some cases, it'll pay to write the question before you ask it.)

For practice in this very important skill, you should construct a number of questions you would like the answers to and ask them of your family members. It will make it easier if you:

1. Follow the listing just given about the decisions you'll have to make before you ask for information.
2. Ask each question only of those members of your family you're sure will know the answer.

ASKING QUESTIONS II

Asking good questions is so difficult that you should practice this skill with your family until you get really good at it. There are questions that are hard for anyone to answer. These would be nice for you to know about. You wouldn't ask such a question of your instructor, but you might ask one of a classmate.

In every class in good schools, there is fierce competition for the few A's that will be given. In every class there will be a sharp student who will look around when the class begins and say to himself: *Okay now, who are the bright ones I have to beat?* This isn't pretty, but it's true. You'll have to defend yourself from these people if you're going to get A's.

Your instructors will know what's going on. In fact, many of them enjoy the competition among their brightest students. It's fun and stimulating to watch good minds at work, so a certain level of competition is encouraged.

When you make statements or answer the instructor's questions, those bright, competitive students in your class working for an A will look for ways to shoot you down (make your answers look less than good). When this happens, if you just fold and let them get away with it, you can kiss you're A grade goodbye. You'll have to defend yourself. One way to do this is to attack right back. A good way to do this is with questions when the sharpie makes his statement.

The idea here is to ask a question that is so complicated that he won't have an easy time following it. The complication doesn't have to be in the context of the question (about the subject), but it can be complicated in structure. If he has to ask you to repeat it, you'll have scored big points, and he may leave you alone the next time. If the sharpie makes a statement similar to this *I believe the world is so much safer now that the Soviet Union has renounced communism that we can, for the most part, disband our army*. You can ask what we call a multi-part question. These are the kinds that you hear asked during presidential press conferences. It might sound similar to this:

> *You say that the world is so much safer now than when there was a central communist control over Russia and her satellites. But this doesn't seem reasonable when: 1) most of the world's destructive power is still in place and operational, and 2) the controls for that power are now so scattered and under so many different forces. My question is a two-part one: 1) What conditions do you see that identify this as a safe situation, and how are they now operating differently than they did a few years ago? and, 2) How can you ignore the two conditions I just mentioned?*

The point here is to ask a question that the sharpie will have to think very hard about to answer but will be prevented from answering it by the complexity of your question. If he has to ask you to repeat a part of the question, you must be able to do so. You can't forget or you lose the point. But, you can do it because you have it written in front of you. He doesn't and has to remember all of the parts. This will be hard even for a sharpie.

You should practice this question-asking with members of your family until you get good at this. At first you'll have to write out the questions to remember them. Soon you'll be able to keep them straight in your head.

ANSWERING QUESTIONS

You'll have to answer questions most of your life. You'll be judged by other people on your intelligence and education by the ways you answer. In order for you to be seen as bright and educated, you'll have to do for other people what I explained teachers have to do for most students who ask questions. You'll have to figure out what the people really want to know and then give them that information.

My wife and I do a lot of traveling telling parents about *Writing Strands* books, and often we find ourselves lost in cities we've never been in before. Even though we carry maps, we have to ask hotel desk clerks for directions. You can see the problems we might have with these examples of typical answers given to us even by people who have jobs where they must direct guests to places in town.

> *This is the first time I've been in this city and I'm late for a meeting. What's the quickest way to the convention center?*

> 1. *Take this road, (wave of the hand) till you get to the first light. . .or maybe it's the second one. . .anyway you'll see a gas station on the corner and turn east. Go about two miles and turn north on the main street. Go clear through town and take the right fork for about three miles. You can't miss it.*

> 2. *The convention center? I think it's just on the other side of town. Over to the north? When you get to town, take the right fork.*

> 3. *The convention center. Let's see, (thoughtful frown). You know the main street in town?*

> 4. *(Speaking very quickly) Turn left and go to Everglade Avenue. Take a right on that till you get to Warren St. Go east two lights till you get to Main St. Go north to the fork. Take a right and you'll be three miles from it. On your left.*

You can see the trouble we might have with these kinds of answers. The clerks hired to help didn't think first about what the situation was, what was known and what information was needed. They didn't hear the important parts of the question we asked: *I'm in a hurry. I'm a stranger to town and I'm lost.*

The clerks answering the questions we asked should have:

1. Given us the address
2. Drawn us a map
3. Given us information slowly enough so that we would have had time to write down the directions

You should ask family members to ask you directions and practice giving them. Keep in mind the points listed as you do so, then ask them to tell you how they plan on finding the places from your directions. This will tell you whether you have or haven't given clear directions.

One way to find out if you've done a good job is to ask them to draw maps of the routes you've just described. If you could follow the maps to the places asked for, then you've done well. If not, figure out where the troubles were in the directions and try again.

REQUEST FOR MORE INFORMATION

There's an old saying: "There are no dumb questions." If you believe this then there's no reason ever not to ask for the information you want. There will be some rules in college, though not written, that you'll be expected to follow. When you want to know something in a college class or in your job, you should:

1. Have been paying attention to what's been going on. Many times students or workers ask questions about material that's just been given to them. If you want to feel really dumb sometime, ask about something that's just been explained. The rest of the class or your co-workers will help you feel that way.
2. Be sure you need the answer. Asking questions just to be participating is another way of being dumb.
3. Be sure you can't find the answer in the usual ways—in the text book or the company manual or directions of operation.
4. Be sure the person you're asking the question of knows the information you want. If not, you're wasting everyone's time.

If you've decided to ask your question, you should first:

1. Know exactly what you want.
2. Phrase the question in your mind before you ask it so that you'll get exactly what you need.
3. Ask the question and then shut up. Don't explain the question or talk about the question.

Don't give the person you're asking questions of choices of answers. This is very irritating to teachers and bosses. Doing so sounds similar to this:

> *Was the major cause of the Civil War the North's desire to free the slaves, or was it the North's desire to preserve the union?*

This limits the person you're asking the question of to those two choices, and maybe that person doesn't like either one and has a third answer. In this case you've wasted everyone's time by giving options, and you've probably irritated almost everyone.

PRESENT IDEAS IN CONTRADICTION TO OTHER'S VIEWS

We all feel we have the right views on topics. (If we didn't we wouldn't have them.) When you're in a classroom situation and views have been given that you don't agree with, you've the right to challenge those views, whether of either the teachers or your classmates.

Good teachers like to have students challenge them as long as the challenges have been well thought out. Don't hold back if you disagree with your teachers. Just make sure you can

22

support your positions. It's no good to say that you disagree just because you don't like what's been said. You have to have good reasons why you disagree. Your teachers will accept your challenges only if you can support them.

Your teachers will expect the bright students in their classes to challenge each other. To make your mark in classes and to get the most out of your time in school, you'll have to work with ideas. Many of them you won't agree with. That's fine; you don't have to. But, when you give an opinion in class, you should expect to have it challenged, and you should be ready to defend it.

Many teachers challenge things the students say just to force them to defend their views. A common device, to get students to discuss ideas, is for teachers to offer ideas that they know the members of the class won't agree with. They'll be asking for the students to challenge their thinking. It will pay you to do so. That's what an education is—exploring ideas.

You should practice challenging ideas so that when they're given to you in class, you'll be able to handle them. Teachers will like it if you phrase your challenges this way:

> *Sir, in your lecture on Tuesday you said that: (At this point you can quote from your notes what the teacher said.). I have a question about that view. I found that the following experts in the field of biology hold a different view. They feel that— (Now you can quote what the other experts feel about the issue.). I would like you to explain why you feel as you do when so many experts in the field think otherwise.*

If you do it this way, it says a number of good things about you to your instructor:
1. You paid attention to and understood the lecture on Tuesday.
2. You were interested enough to do research on the subject and found contrary opinions
3. You're motivated enough to bring up the question in class.
4. You're respectful enough of the instructor to phrase the question in a nice way.

You'll have to be careful while practicing this skill with members of your family. If you don't tell them what you're doing, it's possible your parents might not like to have what they've said questioned, and they might think it strange if you use what other people have said to question what they think.

It might be best if you ask your parents if you can practice your speech work and tell them what you're doing so that they'll understand what your questioning is all about. Your practice sessions might go this way:

> *"Dad, I'd like to practice my speech exercise with you. Is it okay if I ask you some questions about what you said and ask you to explain it?"*
> *"Sure, Son."*
> *"Dad, you said last week that you think it'd be a good idea for there to*

be an independent prosecutor to look into the Whitewater question. But, when there was talk on the TV about a special prosecutor to look into Speaker Gingrich's book deal, you said that that was just politics. Why is looking into questions of ethics in one case good and in another case just politics?"

DEFENDING YOUR IDEAS

In class situations there are always ideas being presented by the instructors and/or the class members. It's never expected that everyone will agree with all of them. Many of them you may find don't fit in with what you believe. That's fine. You can't expect that everyone will always agree on everything. Some of your ideas won't appeal to others in the room either. Your teachers will expect you to be able to defend your ideas and to do so orally in the classroom.

This will be much different than defending your thinking at the dinner table with your family. The other students in the class won't have patience with you trying to explain what you mean.

This isn't easy, but there are some things that you can do that will make this easier.

How you say what you think is very important in defending ideas. This means that the way you defend yourself will determine how effective you'll be in your efforts to defend your ideas.

1. One of the most important things that you can do is to *prepare* to defend what you plan on saying. If you feel that others may not agree with what you plan on saying, then you can expect to be challenged by them. If you have quotations, facts, surveys, or a logical defense prepared in advance, you'll be in much better shape. Those students who challenge what you say won't have an opportunity to prepare an attack on your views. They won't have much to say to you when you present your defense.

   So: A. Expect to have to defend what you say.
       B. Have notes you can refer to in support of what you've said.

2. You'll have a better chance of success if you deal with attacks on your position in a direct and precise way. This means that you'll have to understand what the person has said, see what relationship it might have to your position and respond to that attack and nothing else. An effective way to do this is to repeat the main idea of the attack (using the same words if possible), and then show how that point presented isn't a good one.

   Below is an example of how you might do this in a situation where you've made a point about why America shouldn't have gone to war with Iraq when the Iraqi army invaded Kuwait. With that statement you should get some objections from someone in the class.

24

This objection and your defense could be similar to this:

> *"I think it was wrong of our president to have sent our army to Iraq to help Kuwait."*

You could expect to have someone challenge your thinking on this. It might go this way:

> *"Boy, I don't understand how you figure that. The Iraqi army was taking all the goods in Kuwait and sending them home. They invaded Kuwait and they had no right to do that."*

You can't let this type of an attack succeed. You must defend your position. Remember, that you're to repeat the essence of the position of the attack. It might be similar to this:

> *"I understand that you think that because one country in some far part of the world invades another country that the U.S. should send its army there to interfere. That's an interesting position. This means that you feel that if any country anywhere invades another country that we should declare war with them. I certainly can't agree with that. America can't be the policeman for the whole world."*

TALKING TO GROUPS

Most speech classes are structured with the assumption that when the students are graduated they'll be speaking to fairly large groups of people. Except for a few in occupations such as law, teaching, ministry and politics, this won't happen. The only time most people will have an occasion to speak to more than a few friends will be in township, church or school board meetings. This exercise has been designed to make you more effective at presenting your views to groups.

It will help your practice with this skill if you think of talking to a small group (10 to 30) as you'd think about talking to one person. Many of the principles and techniques are the same. To be effective you must:

1. Show your audience that you like them by:
   A. Smiling
   B. Establishing eye contact
   C. Being open (body stance and gestures)
2. Showing interest in what is important to them
3. Demonstrating confidence in yourself and your subject
4. Requesting reinforcement and acknowledging it

For practice, you could ask to talk to your youth group, scout group, choir, Sunday school class, sport team, homeschooling group or any other group you can use. Most people, if you tell them what you're doing, will be willing to help you practice. If you don't have a group to practice with it makes these skills harder to come by, but not impossible. With imagination you can do much practice. The following list may help you to get started with your exercises:

1. In your mind, create the audience you'll be speaking to.
2. Design your practice talk to that specific group.
3. If possible, use a large room full of chairs to practice. Your church may have rooms that you might use.
4. Prepare what you plan on talking about just as if you were planning on talking to real people.

You should act the same way if you're talking to a group of real or imagined people. All the things you've worked on in this book up to now are important to use. You must:

1. Greet your audience with enthusiasm
2. Show them that you like them
3. Demonstrate to them that you've confidence in yourself
4. Use the body language and eye contact skills you've developed to do these things

Remember: Greet Audience With Enthusiasm

As soon as your audience sees you, you've started to speak to them. You're talking about yourself and your relationship with them as soon as they see:

1. The way you stand
2. Look about
3. Use your facial expressions
4. Hold your arms and hands
5. What you do with your feet

Just as you want to make a good impression with anyone you meet, you'll want to make the same good impression on a group. The techniques for doing so work the same way.

Before beginning practice on these skills, it would pay you to go back over the lessons you've done and make lists of those skills you've mastered. Use that list of skills while working on this exercise. This may seem like lots of busywork and it is time consuming, but you'll find that it'll help you a great deal.

INTERVIEWING

You'll have a number of interviews in your lifetime; some of them may be formal, and others will be more like conversations. How you conduct yourself could be very important to you and will help you to get what you want.

UNDERSTANDINGS

In order to be successful in any interview situation, you must understand three things:
1. You must know exactly what you want from the interview.
2. You must have an understanding of what the person interviewing you wants to know about you and how he or she expects to learn it.
3. You must know how to respond to those techniques to give your interviewer the best possible impression of you.

1. Knowing exactly what you want from an interview is extremely important to both your interviewer and yourself. Keep in mind that an interviewer for a position either owns the company or his or her job is dependent on doing well in selecting the right people to work for the company. Both you and the person you'll be talking to will benefit from you knowing what you want.

Before you interview, it's important that you learn as much as you can about the company and the person or people who run it. The question is bound to be asked of you, *"Why do you want to work for this company?"* If you say, *"I want a job,"* it will be the truth, but it won't impress the interviewer much. How much better for you if you have good reasons for wanting to work there. The following example isn't something you could use, but it'll give you the idea:

> *Sir, my family has lived in this town for almost 100 years, and in that time this company has been one of the main businesses here. Many members of my family have worked here. My grandfather worked in the warehouse in the 50's, my father worked here after he came back from the service, and my older brother worked here during summer vacations to help pay for his college. I have always admired the way this company has treated its employees, and I plan on working here full time when I finish with my education."*

It would be hard for an interviewer not to take such a statement seriously. The point of knowing exactly what you want is important because the interviewer then will recognize

27

that you're one of a rare group of young people who are serious and who know what they want and know how to get it.

It would be good if you knew just what kind of job you want and are qualified for. Rather than saying that you are willing to take any job, you could say that you would like to work in the bookkeeping office, or that you have always wanted to work in the press room. Then it might be important to state that you would be eager to start anywhere.

2. If the person interviewing you is good at the job, he or she will have a small group of people selected from the written applications to interview and from this group will choose who to hire. Your work history, education, qualifications for the job and outside interests will be written in the application which the interviewer will read just before you enter the office. Any questions asked of you about those things will be to see how well you handle yourself and not to get the answers to the questions asked.

Your interviewer will watch how you enter the office, sit, arrange your arms and legs, how you use your eyes and smile, and how you react to questions. He or she will be taking mental notes about how personable you are, how eager and sincere you are, and how well you carry on a conversation.

3. Exercises dealing with the following principles will help you to learn how to satisfy the interests and goals of an interviewer. You should work with family members until you're very comfortable with all of them. Let the people you're working with know what you're trying to do, and they'll be better able to help you.

EXERCISES

These exercises will give you an introduction to the methods you can use to have successful interviews. You should try them one at a time in practice sessions with members of your family and then have someone conduct full interviews with you where you'll have a chance to use all of the techniques at once.

There are a number of principles you should understand before you begin practice interviewing:

1. APPEARANCE

Your age and the type of job or position you're seeking will determine how you should dress. If you're under 15 or 16 years old, no one will expect you to dress like a young business person. What interviewers will want to see is that you've taken some pains to look good for the interviews. They will want to see that you care enough about what you want that you prepared.

2. THE INTERVIEWER

You'll probably be in an office and the interviewer will sit behind a desk for most job interviews. There may be a chair at the side of the desk or in front of it. You shouldn't sit until invited to do so. Your interviewer probably won't leave you standing. If you're left standing, you should try very hard not to shift your feet around, and you should hold your hand and arm movements to a minimum.

Many people, when they're nervous, as you're bound to be, move their arms or hands or feet in a rhythmic manner. Interestingly, it is in time with the beating of a heart. About 70 to 75 times a minute. When you were very young, even before you were born, you took security from the beating of your mother's heart. It is that rhythm that you seek when you're nervous. You must learn to control it, for it's a dead giveaway that you're not comfortable.

When we look at a speaker we don't notice those parts of the body that don't move. If the people we're speaking with don't move their hands, we don't look at them. When we're watching actors on the stage or on TV, if they don't shuffle their feet around, we never look at them. As part of this exercise, turn on the TV and watch how the characters move. What they want you to look at, they'll move. What is unimportant for you to see, they'll keep still.

The principle here is that if you want people you're talking with to look at your hands, move them around, twist your fingers, wring the palms together, bite the nails, or pick at the skin. People will look at your hands. Now you have to decide if their looking at your hands helps you say what you want to or not. If not, keep your hands still. People won't notice them at all. This might feel awkward at first, but you'll get used to it, and you'll be a much more effective speaker because people will look at your face, which is what you want.

3. YOUR ENTRANCE

Your interview will begin as soon as you're seen by the interviewer. When you first walk into the office, you'll be telling the interviewer what kind of person you are and how well you can handle yourself in front of people by the way you stride in, stand, look about, and smile.

If you're seeking a job where you'll be dealing with customers or the public, you should know that the interviewer is looking for a person who:

A. **Smiles**. People like to be smiled at. Remember this. It's important. It says to the people you're talking to that you like them and that you like to look at them. You might practice this around the house.

I can't emphasize this enough. We all like people who smile, and this is very important to employers looking for people to help them deal with the public. There's a big difference between smiling and having an idiot grin on your face. Your practice sessions will help you understand when smiling is appropriate. Your brother or sister might think you're nuts, but smile at them anyway. They might even smile back.

B. **Walks into the room with energy and confidence**. This may be difficult for you. That's why you're working with this book, to give you practice. You might set up a desk and two chairs for a practice office and practice entering. Your parents will help you. What you have to avoid is appearing shy and hesitant. The person looking for a new employee isn't looking for someone who appears scared to be seen or who is so nervous that it's obvious. Sure, you'll be scared and nervous. We all are in new situations. That's why this is important to practice.

Walk right in, and crossing to the desk, hold out your hand and say, *"Good morning, Mr. Jones, I'm Bill Jamison. Thank you for seeing me."* He will shake your hand and ask you to sit. Do so and smile at him and let him start the interview. He may begin with asking you if you had trouble finding his office or the building. Remember, he doesn't care whether you had trouble or not. What he wants to know is how you handle yourself. You might try: *"I didn't have any trouble at all, Mr Jones. The directions your secretary gave me were excellent,"* and then smile at him. He'll like you.

C. **Is able to control body movements**. This doesn't mean that you should be stiff. That won't do at all. It means that you'll have to control your feet and legs so that you're not shifting from one foot to the other, putting one foot on top of the other, standing on one foot, stepping back and forth, crossing and uncrossing your arms or scratching and playing with your hair, and, if you're sitting, swinging your foot or leg.

This may seem silly to you to try and be conscious of these movements. We all had to do this controlling, and you won't realize you have a problem until you practice interviewing with members of your family. You should alert them to watch for this as you practice. If they recognize that you've a problem, you must practice to control yourself. A body out of control isn't what employers want who select employees to deal with the public.

D. **Speaks up!** Many young people, because they're shy or because of previous training or experiences, talk very softly. They're so quiet that they're used to people asking them to speak up or telling them to repeat what they've just said. If this sounds familiar to you, you may need practice in this area.

Many times when I'm in a restaurant or at a motel registration counter, the clerks talk so softly that I have to ask them to repeat themselves. This may be because I'm old, but this also may mean that those people have a problem. This is an easy one to solve. All it takes is practice with your family. Alert them to what you're working on and ask them to tell you when you speak too softly for a "public voice."

E. **Is willing to talk.** Interviewers don't need to ask the questions they do, because they have the interviewees' applications that give them all the answers. What they want to find out from talking to you is to see whether you can carry on a conversation, so they ask you questions that they already know the answers to. If you answer just with a *yes* or *no*, they won't be very interested in having you deal with their customers. This might resemble such an interview between an interviewer (I) and you (Y).

I: *I see here that you were homeschooled.*
Y: *Yes I was.*
I: *Do you think that that experience was as good as getting a diploma from the public school?*
Y: *Yes.*
I: *What about socializing? What was that like?*
Y: *Sure, I did some.*

As you can see, this interviewee wouldn't make a very good impression on someone looking for help in the store, office, factory or restaurant. Notice how much better the following responses sound.

I: *I see here that you were homeschooled.*
Y: *Yes, I was. It was a wonderful experience. I'm very grateful to my parents because they took the time and effort to make sure I got a good education.*
I: *Do you think that your experience was as good as getting a diploma from the public school?*
Y: *I certainly do. I have a very good background in the classics. I have learned two foreign languages. My parents saw to it that I visited museums and art galleries whenever it was possible, in whatever city we were in. And I have scored well above the average in all standardized tests and even the S.A.T.*
    I was even able to take some junior college classes before I finished my high school work. I am very proud of the education my parents made sure I received.
I: *What about socializing? What was that like?*
Y: *That's an interesting point. Many people ask that question and the answer is important. I missed much of the socializing that occurs in the public schools that produces problems for young people. For that I am truly thankful. Plus, I was involved in many of the experiences that have produced real benefits. I was in scouting for nine years. I played on my church hockey, baseball and basketball teams. I took field trips on busses with groups for 11 years. All that plus the work I did with the youth groups in our church makes me feel that I had the best of both worlds and had none of the really bad aspects of socializing.*

31

You can see that this interviewee is more likely to get the job or the appointment. If you tell the members of your family what you're working on and ask them to ask you questions off and on during the day and evening, you'll have lots of opportunity to practice this skill.

When they have asked you questions, make sure they don't let you get away with just a *yes* or *no* answer. The kinds of responses that will be good for interviews will soon become automatic. Your family may even ask you to stop explaining things and answer with short responses. If this happens you'll know that you're ready for an interviewer.

F. **Leaves questions till last that have to deal with how much the job pays.** You'll be expected to ask questions about overtime, insurance, union membership and company activities, such as choirs or sports teams, like bowling or golf. You can also ask about opportunities to work in different departments, so as to learn as much about the business as possible. Don't feel that you shouldn't ask questions like these. It shows that you've thought about it and that you're interested in the work.

What you can't do is start off asking how much you'll be paid. The interviewer will get to that part in time, but you don't want to seem to be most interested in money. He or she will know you expect to be paid and are anxious to know how much.

HOW NOT TO BE A BORE
OR
MAKING OTHER PEOPLE GLAD THEY TALKED TO YOU

This exercise will help you to avoid being boring and help you to understand what it takes to be an interesting conversationalist.

You must have noticed that some people are interesting to talk to and some are really boring. You may remember times when you had short conversations with people whom you had just met, and you were sorry that they have had to end. You may have felt that they were extremely easy to talk with and that they had interesting things to say. Talking with them made you feel important and knowledgeable and the conversations gave you warm feelings. Being able to make others glad that they had a chance to meet and talk with you is something that you can learn and is a skill that is well worth practicing to acquire.

UNDERSTANDINGS

This may not be as hard to understand as you might have thought. The major difference between people who are bores and people who are interesting is in their attitudes toward the people they're speaking with.

There are two principles involved in this not being a bore and in making people glad that they talked with you. The first is an understanding and doesn't take much practice. You just have to keep it in mind. The second involves techniques that take a great deal of practice and, for some people, are hard to master. But, it is so important that, no matter how much work it takes to master the skill, it'll be worth all the time and effort you put into it. These two principles are:

1. A bore is a person who tells other people things that they:
   A. Already know
   B. Can't use
   C. Don't want to learn
2. An interesting person is one who listens to what other people say and is willing to talk about things of interest to them and makes them feel:
   A. Interesting
   B. Knowledgeable
   C. Intelligent

It's easy to identify the first group, the bores. You'll recognize the following bits of conversation and the situations from your experiences with bores. If you recognize yourself somewhat, don't despair. We all have to learn to speak to others without boring them. You're just having your chance to learn that now, if you don't already know.

> You and the bore are standing in the rain. It's running off your hair and down your collar and off the end of your nose. The bore turns to you and says, *"It sure is raining hard."*

There are lots of situations very similar to that one. This is a case of the bore telling you things that you already know and don't need to be told.

How much better if that person had turned to you said, *"Bill, have you ever seen it rain this hard before?"* This would have given you a chance to talk about your experiences, which is what you and all people would like to do.

I had the following conversation with a person I worked with for about fifteen years. He was an avid sports fan. He went to all the school's games, watched all the games he could on TV, and read Sport's Illustrated magazine and the sports pages of the paper every day. He and I would get to the teacher's lounge early every morning and make the coffee. Almost every morning he would tell me about some game he had seen on the weekend or watched on TV. For the first twenty or thirty times he did this, I told him that I didn't follow sports and that I never watched them on TV. He started my day this way for years. You may recognize this:

> *"Dave, did you see the Bear's game last night?"*
> *"No, I don't watch professional sports because they don't interest me."*
> *"You should have seen it. It was one of the best games I've ever seen. At the end of the first quarter. . ."*

This is a case of a bore telling you something you don't want to learn.

Look at the difference in this conversation:

> *"Dave, did you see the Bear's game last night?*
> *"No, I don't watch professional sports because they don't interest me."*
> *"That's strange that you don't enjoy watching. Why is that?"*
> *"It's because I had a chance to be a pro ball player when I was young, and I passed it up to go to college. I'm glad that I did that, but when I watch sports I always feel bad that I missed my chance."*

This response gives Dave a chance to talk about something that's important to him. He certainly wouldn't be bored with the following conversation. If the principles were used, look where it might go:

34

"What sport did you play, Dave?"
"Baseball."
"What position?"
"Pitcher."
"Tell me about the teams you played on."
"I played in high school, semi-pro, for the Air Force and college."
"Wow, you must have been something. What was your best pitch?"
"A fast ball mixed up with a change-up, and we. . ."

You can see that Dave will feel good about this conversation. He gets to talk about himself, which we all like to do, and he doesn't have to listen to someone talk about something he doesn't want to hear about.

You may have had conversations that were similar to this one:

". . .I go to Centerville High. You ever been there?
"No, I homeschool."
"Well, we got the meanest principal you'll ever meet. Watch out for him. If he sees you in the hall during class, it don't matter what reason you got. It's detention."
"I've never been there, and I don't think I'd want to go either."
"Hey, not all the teachers are bad. There's Mr. Danforth. I got him and he's about the best there is. He teaches social studies. If you get him you got it made, gradewise."

This is a case of the bore telling you something you can't use and don't need to know even though you've shown no interest in learning it. The bore knows you don't want to know this information but is willing to use your time telling you because it pleases him.

Look at what happens to this conversation if the principles given in this exercise are observed and used.

". . .I go to Centerville High. You ever been there, Jane?
"No, Alice, I homeschool."
"Hey, that's wild, tell me about what it's like."
"It's just like what you do but I do it at home, that's all."
"But what about books and tests and all that?"
"I have all that, but I do it in a couple of hours instead of all day long."
"That must be nice, being able to stay home and avoid all the hassle of teachers watching you all the time. But, don't you miss the kids?"
"No, I see lots of kids. Just last week. . ."

You can see the difference here and what effect it would have on Jane's feelings about the conversation. Alice doesn't talk about what she's interested in. She doesn't talk about things that Jane has no interest in. And, she doesn't give Jane information that she can't use.

It's easy to recognize bores because they talk only about things that are of interest to themselves. If you examine their conversations, you'll see that they make no attempt to find out what's interesting to the people they're talking at. Yes, they talk *at* people not *with* them. They have their interests and don't care what other people are interested in.

It's easy to recognize their speech patterns because most of their sentences begin with the word *I*. Some people can't talk without starting every sentence with that word, and with every subject that's brought up, they talk about themselves. You may recognize the following:

> *"Hi, Jane. Sorry I'm late, but we just got back from the mall."*
> *"It looks like you got the same kind of shoes I have, Betty. But, hey, I bet I paid less than you did. I got mine on sale at Sears last week. Me and my mom went and spent the day. I really like 'em. They're sharp. I'm going back and see if they have anything more I like this weekend."*

Instead of letting Betty tell her about her new shoes she has just bought, Jane starts right off telling Betty about what a bargain she had gotten when she bought hers. Betty probably is excited about her new clothes, but she doesn't get a chance to talk about them at all. Instead of letting Betty feel good about this conversation, Jane creates the situation where she uses Betty's time to make herself feel good.

MAKING OTHER PEOPLE GLAD THEY TALKED TO YOU

UNDERSTANDINGS

To feel good about employing your skills at pleasing other people when you talk with them, you'll have to accept that this isn't manipulation of others for your gain. What you'll be doing is giving other people the chance to feel good about themselves. Another way to look at is that you're letting them use you to help them feel good about talking to you.

There are two principles that you should be familiar with before you do the exercises. They are that people:

1. Like to talk about themselves
2. Like to talk most about things that interest them.

This makes people sound self-centered, but that's what most of us are. You can use that understanding of people's self-interest to make them glad they had a chance to talk with you.

One of the most important things that you can do is to eliminate the word *I* from your conversations. This is really hard, but practice will allow you to do it. What will happen is that you'll end up not talking about yourself—which is what you should want to happen. When you're in conversations with others and you don't use *I*, the conversations will deal with the things that are of interest to your conversational partners. This will make them glad to be talking to you.

To give you an example of how effective this is, you might read the play *Harvey*. There's a character named Elwood Dowd in it who spends his days talking to other people. The author understood the importance of the principle that you'll be working with. When in these conversations, Dowd rarely uses the word *I*, and he really listens to what the people he is in conversations with say. Reading this play will give you a good understanding of the power you'll have if you employ this principle.

Most people don't listen to other people when they talk. They're thinking ahead to what they'll say when they get the chance to talk. They're interested in what they want to say and not in what they're hearing. The people they're talking with know this, but they're doing the same thing. We pretend that this isn't the case, but, if you listen carefully when your friends and family members are talking, you'll recognize this at work.

Your days will run a lot smoother if you don't mention what you know about this around the house.

EXERCISES

To do these exercises, you'll have to force yourself to have lots of conversations. They don't have to be with your family or friends; they can be with anyone. It might be best not to use family, anyway. You can talk to the bag boy at the grocery story, the attendant at the gas station, the crossing guard at the corner after the public school lets out, the clerk at the drug store, the librarian or any people you meet at any time and place. A good way to start these conversations is to ask questions you're sure they'd know the answers to. The example below should help you to understand how they might sound:

> *"How long you been selling papers on this corner?"*
> *"About 15 years now."*
> *"You must have seen almost every person who lives in this part of town by now. You got regular customers? Ones who stop every day to get a paper?"*
> *"Sure I do. I bet I know almost everybody's name that buys papers from me. Lots of 'em know me by name, too. They come up and say, `Hi, Harry, how ya doing?' I say `Morning, Mr. Rottinni, how're you today?'"*
> *"That's interesting. You really like your job, don't you?"*
> *"Oh yeah, I'd rather be doing this than. . .*

Notice that the person talking to Harry doesn't use *I* once. You can be sure Harry likes this conversation, because he gets to talk about himself and what he likes to do. You should have conversations like this where you deal with what others like to think and talk about.

When I was doing my graduate work in speech at Central Michigan University, I got to play Elwood Dowd in *Harvey,* the play I suggested you read. Trying to get into the mood and actions of the character, I spent lots of time talking to strangers, much as Dowd does in the play. I used the techniques Dowd uses, the ones listed in this lesson, and I found that people really liked talking to me. In fact, I found that I had to keep from talking to people, because, when I did, they would follow me around. I was really amazed at how much power I had over other people's attention.

When I was teaching these techniques to high school and college students, they often would ask me how to cut conversations short, because the people they were working with enjoyed talking with them so much that they couldn't get away from them. This may happen to you too.

If you get good at this, you'll have to be careful that you treat others with care and kindness. When we have the chance to control others, we have the responsibility to care for their feelings. You'll recognize, when using these techniques, that the people you're talking with will enjoy talking with you so much that they'll want to keep right on talking with you. This will be because most people never have conversations where the people they're talking with really listen to what they have to say and respond to it. They'll enjoy talking with you so much that you'll have to find kind ways to break off the conversations.

Before you practice having conversations without using the word *I*, you should have conversations with people you know and keep records (they may just be in your head), about the frequency of their use of *I*. If you can do it without embarrassing anyone, you might use a tape recorder to give you a better record. I have the feeling you're going to be surprised at how often *I* is used, even by yourself.

Once you are convinced that most people like to talk about themselves and things that are of interest to them, you should start your exercises where you talk to people controlling your use of *I* and talking about things that they like and want to talk about.

As you do this, you should respond to what people say to you with evident interest. This means that when they tell you something you should:

1. Nod.
2. Smile.
3. Say, "yes," or "Uh huh."
4. Look into their eyes.

When they've made a point, or when they've answered your question, you should indicate to them that you're interested in what they're saying and that you want to hear them talk about it more. You can do this if you:

1. Ask them to explain by saying *"That's not clear, can you explain that to me?"*
2. Ask them to talk more about that by saying *"Would you talk more about that, it's really important to me."*
3. Say *"That's interesting,"* or *"Why is that,"* or *"You really feel strongly about that, don't you?"* or *"That's an unusual reaction or feeling. Tell me why you feel that way."*

What you're doing here is saying to them, "I think that you're an interesting person and I enjoy talking to you."

This may be the hardest exercise you do, but it can be one of the most important for you. Practice it until you feel that you're good at it. Then, use this skill you will have developed with care. Remember that you'll be controlling the emotional reactions of others, and you then become responsible for how they feel about that experience. Treat their feelings with care. Keep in mind that this is a very powerful tool that you're learning. Not many people your age have this skill. You'll find you have a lot of power over other people when you get good at it. You might talk with your parents about whether they think you're ready for this yet.

It may seem to you that I'm going over this point too much, but that's on purpose. Once you get good at this skill, you'll have a tremendous power over others when you're in conversations. You won't like yourself if you abuse that power.

I CAN TOP THAT

This is another technique that's hard for some people to learn. It has to do with giving to other people the credit and the feelings about themselves that they want. I think one of the reasons that it's hard for some is that the people using this technique have to feel very secure about themselves in order to make the people they're talking with feel important, bright, knowledgeable or right. You can't do that if you feel the need to make yourself look important or right.

UNDERSTANDINGS

You'll have to decide whether it's more important to you to be right or to make the people you're talking with feel good about themselves. Most of the time you can't do both things. An example may help make this clear. Suppose that your friend says that a few years ago The Bulls took the NBA championship three years running. Now you know that this isn't true. You have to decide what to say.

If you say *"No, that's not right. The Bulls have never won three straight years, and I'll bet you I'm right."* You might win the bet. You might feel good about being right, and you might end up able to demonstrate that you know more than your friend does. But your friend won't feel good. Your friend won't enjoy talking with you as much nor feel as comfortable talking with you. What do you want? You can't have both situations—proving you're right and making your friend feel good.

You could say *"I didn't know that. I've never heard that the Bulls were that good. That must have been an exciting three years."*

What happens now is that your friend has enjoyed being right and knowing more than you do about the Bulls' history. Has it hurt you to let your friend think this? Of course not. Has it changed what you know about professional basketball? Of course not. What it has done is allowed your friend to feel good about himself in his enjoyable conversation with you.

EXERCISES

This technique can be used in lots of situations. Suppose your friend, Sally, comes home from college for Christmas and her parents surprise her with a car to take back to school. It's three years old but that doesn't matter to Sally, because she loves it. She's all excited when she calls you to see if you can go for a ride with her.

Your parents have given you a new car for Christmas. What do you do when Sally calls and says *"Guess what I got for Christmas. My own beautiful, little car!"* You can ruin her day by saying *"That's nice but my parents just gave me a brand new VW Bug."* This won't make you feel good because it'll make Sally feel so bad. She was really excited to share with you the surprise and wonder of having her own car, and you ruined it by telling her about yours.

How much better if you were to say *"Oh, Sally, that's just wonderful! What color is it?. . . When can I get to ride in it?. . . Can I ask my dad to drop me off at your house so we can try it out?"*

Sally will eventually learn that you were given a new car the same Christmas that she got her used one, but she'll always love you because you didn't ruin her Christmas by telling her. What would you rather have, the fun of telling Sally about your car or the fun of doing such a nice thing for your friend?

You'll have lots of opportunities to practice this technique. You'll find that the more you use it, the more people will tell you about themselves. They won't feel that you'll put them down by topping what they say.

Think about these situations:

Your friend says *"I got a B+ in math class!"* and you got an A. What do you say?

Your friend says *"We went to the Y.M.C.A. pool this last weekend and had a great time,"* and you went with another friend to their cottage at the lake. What do you say?

Your little brother says *"I saw the full moon last night. I think I saw a face in it. It was really neat,"* and you've been studying astronomy for the last six months. What do you say?

If you look for opportunities to make people glad that they shared their joys with you, you'll find lots of them. It'll make you happier if you're generous with other people.

YOU BECOME WHAT YOU PRETEND TO BE

This is not really a speech exercise, but, it does involve an important aspect of interpersonal relationships. The principles presented here can even be used with people other than members of your family.

It comes as a surprise to most kids when they realize that their parents have wanted for them, for the most part, many of the same things that they've wanted for themselves. They just wanted these things at different times.

All kids want to be seen as ready for responsibility and to be seen as serious youngsters by their parents. Just as parents want their children to be ready for and to take on more responsibility.

UNDERSTANDINGS

You can understand what your parents want from you and what they would like to be able to expect of you. Once you do, you can perform in ways that will indicate to your parents that you're ready for the kinds of responsibilities that you want and that they would like to give you.

Once you know what they would like to expect of you, you can decide what you'll have to do to convince them that you're ready for more responsibility (freedom). Of course, you'll have to be reasonable in your expectations. You wouldn't expect to drive the car without a license, or at fourteen, to be allowed to take a train alone to New York to visit your friends. But, you might expect to be given more choices about what clothes to buy, what and when to study, what to play on the radio, who to visit, and how to wear your hair. Or, if you're older, you might be given more choices about using the family car, places for vacations, friends, curriculum to use, and college plans.

It might be hard for you to believe it, but these are just the things that your parents are anxious for you to make decisions about. They just have to be convinced that you're mature enough to make judgments that will be good for you and reflect well on the rest of the family.

This is your job—to convince them that you're ready for the decisions that you want to make. This is a lot easier than you might think. All you have to do is make a list of the things that your parents ask you to do over and over again. It might read similar to this:

1. Pick up the dirty clothes in my room and put them in the clothes hamper.
2. Help with the dishes.
3. Put tools away after I use them.
4. Make my bed and clean up my room.
5. Return library books on time.
6. Turn off the lights when I leave a room.
7. Shut the door after I go through it.
8. Come home when I say I will.

I'm sure you can come up with a much longer list for yourself. These then are the things that you should be doing on your own, but your parents have to ask to do them over and over again. This can be the solution to your problem of your parents feeling you're not responsible enough.

Put this list on your mirror and check it every day to make sure that you've done these things before anyone has had the chance to ask you to do them.

Soon your mother will say to your father:

> *You know, Bob, Janet must be growing up. I haven't had to ask her in over two weeks to help with the dishes, pick up her room or put her dirty clothes in the hamper. It's really a relief to see her becoming so responsible.*

If this were to happen, then when you ask to do something that your parents have not been sure you've been responsible enough to do in the past, they'll have to see you in a new way. Listen to them think:

> *Janet's growing up. She's showing much more responsibility than she had been. . .really shaping up. Now that she's more mature, maybe I should let her do some of the things she's been asking to do.*

I learned this technique when I was about 15 years old and living with my parents. I had just gotten my driving license, but I wasn't getting the car to drive much at all. All my friends got to drive their family car, but not me. I felt sorry for myself for a bit then made an attempt to analyze the problem, because it wasn't going away. I hit on this technique.

I began washing the car every three or four days. When I did get to drive with my parents in the car, I would insist on putting some gas in it and paying for it myself. I started offering to help with the dishes without the usual fight. I started mowing the lawn without being asked. I waxed the car! In those days there weren't the quick waxes like there are now. It was Simonize (That's a hard wax that takes hours to buff to a shine). I even cleaned the garage.

One day, not too long after I started this process of convincing them that I was getting mature

43

attitudes, my dad handed me the keys and said, "Son, why don't you take the car and visit your friends this afternoon?"

The surprising thing is that I had gotten into the habit of doing the lawn and the dishes without being asked. The joke was on me—I *was* growing up.

If you try this technique, I think you'll find that it works. Many people say we are the kind of people we act like we are, and not the people we say we are. In this case, you'll be acting like a mature young person. That means that if you keep it up, you'll become a mature young person. Mature young people get to make more decisions for themselves than do immature young people. Think about it, anyway.

UNDERSTANDING OTHER PEOPLE'S POINTS OF VIEW

UNDERSTANDINGS

This is an exercise in seeing things from other people's points of view. Sometimes this is called empathy—understanding other's feelings. There's very little of this in our culture. For some reason this skill isn't taught in the schools, and so most parents weren't trained in this, unless they learned this skill from their parents. So, most parents don't understand how to pass this on to their children. The churches teach this, but many of us don't apply the principles we're exposed to.

The result is that most of us sit apart and look at the rest of the people in the world as separate entities, and we look at them with very little understanding of what they may be feeling, thinking or what they want and need.

Before you start this exercise, you might get from your library John Donne's sermons and find "No Man Is An Island." He tells us that we're all part of the same body of man, and that the fate of each of us is connected to all the rest of us. He ends with the idea that the ringing bell doesn't call just some of us but that when it rings, it rings for each of us. "Do not ask for whom the bell tolls, it tolls for thee."

You can't understand this concept until you have the ability to see things through the eyes of other people. That's what this exercise is designed to help you to do.

It would be best if you were to work first with members of your family. Your mother and father should be eager to help you understand how empathy works.

EXERCISES

For these exercises to do you any good at all, you'll first have to decide that you want to know how other people feel about things that you're involved in. When you do something dumb, how does your mother feel about it? What does she mean when she talks to you about what you've done? How does she see your actions? (This means how important does she feel that they are.)

The only way you can understand these things is to look at you from her eyes. That means that you'll have to pretend that you're the mom and that she's the you.

To do this, you and your mother have to agree to change roles for the exercise. You'll have to pretend that you (your mother) has done something dumb and your mother (you) has to tell you how dumb it was and to tell you how to avoid doing it again.

This can be anything that you (really you) have done in the past.

1. Dropped the dinner plates because you tried to carry too many from the table to the sink
2. Talked so long on the phone that the rest of the family couldn't get the calls that were important to them
3. Left your dirty clothes on the floor in your bedroom
4. Left your books on the hall table for about the thousandth time
5. Hung your coat over the back of a chair instead of putting it away in the closet
6. Not shut the door or turned off the lights
7. Stood in front of the open refrigerator thinking about what you'd like
8. Drunk milk directly from the bottle

You could use some of these for this exercise or any of the hundreds of things that all parents have to talk to all kids about again and again.

There will be two parts to this exercise:

1. The two of you will reverse roles and act like the other person has been acting in dealing with the dumb act.
2. The two of you will reverse roles and act like you would like the other person to act in dealing with the dumb act.

PART ONE   (how you think the other party has been acting toward the situation)

Once you have chosen an action and before you reverse roles, you and the other person (your mom) should agree on some ground rules. For instance, you should agree not to:

1. Mock the speech or actions of the other person.
2. Be sarcastic.
3. Treat the exercise as a joke or try to be funny. This will ruin the effect of the reversal. It's quite possible that you and your mom will ending up laughing about yourselves and the situation, but that's an entirely different thing.
4. Say things that will be belittling of the other person or use gross exaggeration to make a point.
5. Do things that the other person doesn't do.

You should agree to:

1. Be serious in your attempt to act, talk, and gesture like the other person.
2. Try to have the attitude of the other person about the dumb act.

PART TWO: (how you think the situation should be handled by both parties)

Before you and your partner reverse roles you should agree not to:

1. Be sarcastic in trying to be nice to each other (This will only benefit you if it's done realistically.)
2. Change in any major way the relationship that you and your partner have established in the past

You should agree to:

1. Be reasonable about what you'd like to have happen. (When this is all over and you both go back to being who you really are, you'll still be the child and your mom will still be a mother who has a whole family to take care of.)
2. Make a real attempt to understand the limitations of personality and character that you're both working with. (Your mom will have to understand that when this is all over you'll still be who you are and will still be as likely to forget things as you always have been.)

You might work on this exercise with as many members of your family as will be willing to work with you. This is especially important for the male members, because this is something that boys and men don't understand very well. For some reason, in our culture it's not considered important for men to feel the pain other people are feeling. I think it has to do with desires for masculinity. "Men don't cry" or something like that.

Keep in mind that the point of this practice is not to get you to do the dishes without being asked. The point is that you can learn something about empathy. Only when we can feel the joy and pain other people feel can we understand their actions.

HOW TO DISAGREE

It's important that members of a family learn to disagree and still retain the love and respect they have for each other. No one expects all people to agree on everything. If people did agree on every subject, it would be either a perfect world or a very dull one.

We don't have a perfect world and it's certainly not a dull place to be. There's an old Chinese curse that says: "May you live during interesting times." This curse means that when things run smoothly, sometimes it's not exciting. The curse means that if an enemy were to live in interesting times that there would have to be lots of discord, strife and disruption to life.

This doesn't mean that disagreement between family members or friends has to be traumatic. Feelings don't have to be hurt because people don't think alike. There are ways to disagree with each other and still feel good and secure in relationships.

There's a big difference between disagreement and contradiction. Don't get them mixed up or you'll live in interesting times. Contradiction is when your dad says something and you say, *"No it's not,"* or *"It is so."* This isn't smart or good to do, and sometimes it can even be painful.

UNDERSTANDINGS

You'll have a better relationship with people you disagree with if you recognize that we all need to feel that:

1. Our thinking is good.
2. Our attitudes are sound.
3. Our positions are valid.
4. Our opinions are respected.

If you already understand that it's more important to protect these four things for the people you're in disagreement with than with your being right about the position you might have on any issue or subject, you won't need to do this exercise at all. If this is the case, both you and your family are very fortunate and very rare. Most people never think about the needs we all have to feel.

This means that when most of us get into disagreements, we say and do things that tend to destroy the feelings others need to have about themselves.

EXERCISE

You can work with members of your family on this skill, and after some practice, your relationships won't suffer when you and others disagree.

You and your partner should pick a subject that you disagree about. You both should write your position down so that it's clear to both of you. For instance:

> You: *I feel that a fourteen-year-old boy should be able to have a motor scooter if he can buy it with his own money.*
>
> Mother: *I don't think fourteen-year-olds are mature enough to drive a motor scooter on the road no matter who buys it.*

This kind of disagreement can end up with the boy saying things such as:

1. "You never let me do anything I want to."
2. "All the other kids have motor scooters, but you don't trust me."
3. "You just want me to stay a little kid forever."

And the parent saying things such as:

1. "There's no need to go on like this. You're not getting a motor scooter and that's that."
2. "If you keep this up this way, you'll lose your bicycle, too."
3. "You're not getting one and that's final," and, "Because I say so and I'm your mother."

In this example, if the principles were applied, it doesn't mean that the boy would get his motorbike or that he wouldn't want one anymore. If his mother didn't want him to have one, he wouldn't get one. What it means is that he would still feel that his **thinking was good**, his **attitude was sound**, his **position (wanting a motorbike) was a valid thing to want,** and that his mother still **respected his opinion**.

In this exercise, you both should keep in front of you a paper on which you've listed the four things that we all need to feel about ourselves:

Keep in mind as you work with skill, every one of us needs to feel that:

1. Our **thinking is good**.
2. Our **attitudes are sound**.
3, Our positions are valid.
4. Our **opinions are respected**.

You should agree on who should start the disagreement. It doesn't matter, except that sometimes the subject will determine who should begin. It would make no sense if your mother woke you up one morning and started telling you that you couldn't have a motorbike when you'd never even asked for one.

You must agree that you both will listen to all of the statements the other person makes and not ever interrupt. This is very important for both parties. Many times parents feel that the positions their children have are not worth listening to, and they have a tendency to cut them off with a hurried "No." or "That's enough, now. I don't want to hear any more about this." Teenagers have a tendency to want to interrupt their parents with more arguments.

There should be some ground rules agreed upon by both parties before you start the disagreement:

1. Don't belittle the other person.
2. Don't directly contradict.
3. Don't get personal.
4. Never bring up, in a negative way, things like short-comings that might be painful to the other person.
5. Allow the other person to save face.
6. Suggest alternatives.

With these ground rules, have at it. I think that you'll find that you both will be doing a lot more listening to the other person's view than you have been in the past.

Think about the different reactions your friend might have if you were in a disagreement and you handled yourself by ignoring this exercise and following these rules of disagreement:

WITHOUT FOLLOWING THE RULES

Friend: *I think the Republican plan for the budget is a really good idea, and I hope it passes.*

You: *That's the dumbest thing I ever heard you say. I can't see how anyone could think like that.*

Friend: *Okay, you're so smart, what's wrong with it?*

You: *A whole bunch of stuff. What about the Clean Water Act? What about the forests they want to cut down? What about feeding hungry kids? What about taking care of old people? What about the poor? Didn't you ever think about this at all?*

Friend: *You always talk like you know everything and you just don't understand anything! If you knew anything about politics at all, you'd know that. . . .*

You can see that this exchange, not an unusual one, would violate the feelings of both people.

50

FOLLOWING THE RULES

> **Friend:** *I think the Republican plan for the budget is a really good idea, and I hope it passes.*
>
> **You:** *That's an interesting view. Tell me why you feel that way.*
>
> **Friend:** *A whole lot of reasons. I care about small businesses, the economy, the dumping that foreign steel makers are doing and I like the idea of paying smaller taxes. I think these things will be taken care with the Republican budget?*
>
> **You:** *I do, too. Just like you do. But I feel that much of the talk about these things is the result of politics. These politicians just want to get re-elected and so they'll say anything to get what they want. What I believe is. . .*

Being able to disagree this way will take lots of practice. It's a very mature way of looking at things. I'm sure your parents will be happy to help you with this exercise. You both should enjoy it. It was lots of fun when my son, Corey, was home with us and we had disagreements. We learned to really enjoy the discussions we had. We often ended up still in disagreement, but we never felt badly toward each other because of them.

HOW TO REDUCE AGGRESSION

All of us, at some time or an other, have displeased those people we're responsible to, or those we love, or those who have the job of training us. It's got to happen.

When it does, there are ways for us to reduce the feelings toward us that we might think of as aggressive. In the case of your parents, even when you do the really dumb things that we all do, they still love you, and the actions they take and the things they say at those times are partly because they're disappointed in you and are partly their efforts to help you to understand what you've done and to make it easier for you to avoid doing those things again.

This is painful for all the people involved. You can lessen the anxiety this might cause by the way you react to being corrected.

UNDERSTANDINGS

This exercise is not designed to allow you to save face, boost your ego, get the best of anyone, pull any fast tricks or get away with anything. It presents the techniques you can use to defuse a situation or lesson the tensions between whoever is being aggressive and yourself.

If you can accept that when the situation is back to normal that that person will still be your parent, boss or instructor, or friend, and that you will still have to live and/or work together, you can understand how these techniques can be valuable. The best thing that could happen between the two of you is that you wouldn't repeat the things that started the aggression, and that the other person would feel that the problem is solved and won't occur again. It would be best for all if this solution could be reached without anyone having hard feelings.

When you've done something dumb and you employ these techniques, the person you're with should feel that you've handled the situation well.

1. To reduce the aggression (and the pain) in these situations you must understand:
    A. How your parent, friend, boss, or instructor feels
    B. What they want
    C. Why they're being aggressive with you

2. You must not defend your actions that caused the problem. You must:
    A. Admit that your actions were wrong or dumb.
    B. Agree that your parent, friend, boss or instructor is justified to be dissatisfied with your actions.

52

C. State that you'll make every effort not to repeat the error.

D. Be sincere in thanking the person for bringing the error to your attention and mention that you appreciate the help you've been given in understanding the situation. (Be careful here. This could be seen as being smart or sarcastic if you're not sincere. If you say these things and you don't mean them, it could make the situation worse.)

The following examples will help you see the difference between the typical response a young person might make to being criticized and one where these techniques are employed.

Typical Response

Father: *John, I see that you've left your bike in the drive again. I had to park out on the street. I've asked you over and over again not to do that. What's it going to take to get you to do what I ask?*

John: *I just came in for a drink of water. I'm going right out again.*

Father: *I don't care how long you're going to be in the house. That's not the point. The point is that I've told you not to leave your bike in the drive.*

John: *Well, you won't let me park it on the lawn. You won't let me leave it on the sidewalk and I can't leave it in the street. What am I supposed to do when I want to come in for a minute, hang it up in the garage?*

Father: *Don't give me smart answers. Just do as I ask, or I'm going to take that bike and put it away till you get some sense of responsibility.*

John: *Just because I wanted a drink?*

Father: *That's it! The bike is off the street for a week. Put it in the garage now and leave it there tell next Saturday.*

John: *That's not fair!*

What happens here is that John has done a dumb and irresponsible thing that he's often been warned about in the past. He then defends his actions, even though he knows that he's wrong. By doing this, he challenges his father's authority, and his father can't allow that to happen without a response, and it's a typical one. The bike is put away.

Analysis

Look at this listing of attack responses in this exchange:

1. Adult confronts (attacks) youth. *(complains about bike in drive)*
2. Youth defends actions. *(makes excuse for bike in drive)*
3. Adult feels that his authority is challenged. *(son shows that he doesn't recognize father's request as reasonable)*
4. Adult feels that he must escalate aggression with threat. *(to put bike away)*

5. Youth calls threat unrealistic. *("Just because. . ."*
6. Adult must now apply threat. *(bike is put away)*
7. Youth complains about punishment. *(if adult again is threatened by this reaction, the punishment is increased until resistance is squashed.)*

The same sequence of actions and responses may occur with any two people when one is in a position of authority and one has done something dumb. It could be a boss or a supervisor and an employee, a teacher and a student, any adult in the care of any child, and it works the same way even with a police officer and any motorist who has been caught speeding or making a rolling stop at a stop sign.

It might pay you to go over in your mind the last time you were criticized for doing something you shouldn't have done. List the events (do it on a piece of paper), much as I have done here. Examine the listing. See if you recognize your reactions in some past situation.

A More Appropriate Response

The same situation follows—the bike has been left in the drive. But, this time John employs this aggression-reduction technique.

Father: *John, I see that you've left your bike in the drive again. I had to park out on the street. I've asked you over and over again not to do that. What's it going to take to get you to do what I ask?*

John: *Oh, boy. You're right, Dad. I did it again. I'm really sorry about this. I'll go out and move it into the garage right now.*

Father: *Now wait a minute. I want to make sure this doesn't happen again.*

John: *I do too. I'm going to tie a piece of bright yarn on the handlebars to remind me. I hope that works. I'm sorry I forgot, Dad. I'll try really hard not to leave it in the drive again. Thanks for being patient with me about this.*

Father: *Well. . . okay. Thanks, Son.*

Analysis

Again, look at the listing of responses in this similar exchange, but notice the differences in the father's reactions:

1. Adult confronts (attacks) youth. *(complains about bike in drive)*
2. Youth admits error, tells adult that the adult is right, apologizes and offers to move the bike right then. *(does not defend action or make excuse)*
3. Adult asserts authority. *(doesn't want to let youngster get away free of criticism)*
4. Youth reduces aggression in adult by agreeing with him that it can't happen again and offers suggestion about tying yarn to bike to help him remember. He then thanks the adult

54

for being patient with his mistakes. *(this makes it almost impossible for the adult to continue being aggressive)*

This resolution to this adult-teenager situation is much smoother than the first one. The results for the father are that:

1. The father understands that the son recognizes his error and doesn't feel that his authority has been questioned.
2. The father doesn't feel badly toward his son, because he understands that the son is young and forgets things.
3. The father respects the son's effort to solve the problem.
4. The father feels that the son won't commit the error again, and further, the father is pleased that he's good at handling situations with his son so well.

The resolution for the son in this situation is that:

1. The son is not punished.
2. The son does not have a father who is mad at him.
3. The son has a chance to solve the problem himself.
4. The son feels that his father respects him for his attitude and that their good relationship is maintained.

Keep in mind that if this technique is used by the son, it's not a process of the son manipulating his father, because one of the main points of the technique is that the son has to be sincere to make this work as it should. If you use this technique, and I recommend that you do, be very sure you mean exactly what you say. If you do, you'll find that things will go very smoothly for you, but only if you do what you say you will.

EXERCISES

1. You should write a script similar to the example I just gave you. Of course, it should be longer and contain more detail. It should be between you and one of your parents or your boss or some instructor. It should have you doing something dumb and have the adult correct your actions. In this script, apply the principles of this technique to your responses to being criticized. This will lock into your mind the principles and how they work.

2. Once you feel that you thoroughly understand this technique, set up such a situation with one of your parents to practice. Explain what you're trying to learn. You might even have them read this exercise so that you're sure they understand what you're doing. This time you won't have a script. You'll have to make it up as you go along.

You might have to do this three or four times before you're sure you have it down right.

3. Now it's just a matter of waiting. Soon you're going to do something dumb. There's no way to avoid it. We all do dumb things. This will be the test for you. Can you reduce the aggression when you're caught doing the dumb thing?

Of course, your parents will recognize what you're doing, because they've worked with you on it. That won't make any difference if you're sincere in what you say and do. You both should have so much fun with this experience that, right in the middle of you getting bawled out, the whole family might just burst out laughing.

APPENDIX

SPEAKING WITH BODY LANGUAGE

This body language section doesn't have a suggested, specific exercise, but it may help you communicate and understand what others are saying to you by the ways bodies are used.

The power of this type of communication was made very clear to me years ago when I was at the Lincoln Park Zoo with my wife and son, Corey. He was about two-and-one-half years old.

We went to see the new primate exhibit. They had recently installed a large glass enclosure where they held orangutans. I had just finished a book about communication between primates and was eager to try some of the techniques out on one of the great apes. My wife, holding Corey, and I stood looking through this thick glass cage at a huge female.

Apes don't look each other in the eye because that's seen as an act of aggression. They glance at each other and quickly look away. I did this with the orangutan. For about five minutes I looked at her then quickly away. I noticed her looking at me. She would glance briefly at me then look off across the cage at something of great interest. Every once in a while our eyes would connect. I realized with great joy that she was "talking" back to me. We were telling each other that we weren't being aggressive with each other.

When apes want to be groomed, and this is important to them, for it keeps them clean and reduces parasites, they have a ritual they go through. They establish eye contact. They go through the procedure this orangutan and I had just established. They pretend to groom themselves, glancing at each other occasionally. They do this by picking at bits of skin on their arms and putting the bits of skin in their mouths. I started this procedure. I would pick at my arm and pretend to put what I had found in my mouth. I kept glancing at her, and soon she began to pick at her fur and put bits into her mouth, glancing up at me every two or three seconds or so. This was very exciting for me. We were now having a conversation!

When they have established that they both are interested in a grooming session, apes can approach each other without fear that they'll be seen as aggressive. I reached out to the glass wall and pretended to groom her. She must have seen this as my interest, for she approached the glass. Stopping just a foot away, she watched my actions for a few minutes with much pursing of her lips. She picked at the glass on her side as if offering to groom me. We ended up with both of us picking at each other through the glass wall just as if we were grooming each other.

We ended up with her huge nose pressed flat against the glass on her side and me with my nose pressed against the glass on my side, and our eyes about two inches apart. I was having this great relationship with a seven-hundred pound orangutan. They have beautiful brown eyes.

The point in telling you this story, other than that it was fun, is to show you that other animals communicate with the members of their species with body language. People have spoken language, but like the other animals, we also talk to each other with our bodies.

The ways we sit, stand, walk, hold our shoulders, cross our legs and arms, hold or twist our hands and use our facial muscles tell other people how we feel about them or ourselves or the situations we're in.

Just as with spoken language, there are two elements to body language. There is the delivery and the reception of the message. To get any message from one person to another, both the sender and the receiver of the message must have the same body vocabulary. This lexicon of body messages has to be learned.

Some body messages are different if the cultures are not the same. A message sent in New York might not be understood in Togo, Africa. But there are some universal body signals that are the same for all cultures. All people seem to react in much the same way to surprise, distress, contempt, shame, fear, interest, joy, disgust and anger. All people are programmed to smile when they're happy, turn their mouths down when they're displeased, and go through a lot of the same facial gestures, such as wrinkling the forehead, lifting the eyebrow, or raising one side of the mouth.

There are examples of very different body vocabularies. For instance, in our country we shake our head from side to side to say no, and nod up and down to say yes. But in India these gestures have just the opposite meanings. Side to side means yes and up and down means no. You can get a very interesting reaction from a friend who has asked you a question if you answer yes at the same time you shake your head from side to side, or say no as you nod. You're sending confusing and contradictory messages and you'll be able to see the confusion on the other person's face.

Below are some of the ways we talk with our bodies in our culture. These don't always mean the same thing, but generally:

* When we don't believe something someone has said, we let them know it by lifting one eyebrow.

* When we're feeling insecure or wish to be isolated from others, we hold our arms about our bodies.
* When we feel indifference (we don't care), we shrug our shoulders.
* When we want to tell someone that we both know something that others don't know, or we wish to establish a special bond, we wink one eye.
* When we have strong negative feelings about something someone has said, we push the statement or the idea away from us with our hands, much as we would push a grocery cart out of our way.
* When we don't accept what someone is saying, we cross our arms over our chests or cross our legs.
* When we wish to say to people that we can't believe what's happening to us, or that we have just witnessed something really dumb, we roll our eyes upward.
* When we wish to have someone accept something we've said, we open our arms with our palms facing upwards.
* When we're impatient, we tap fingers or rock one foot.
* When we've forgotten something and want to let others know that we're feeling stupid about it, we slap our foreheads.
* When we want someone to continue talking or explaining something to us, we gesture with our hands as if we were asking them to come closer.
* When we don't understand something, we tend to rub our noses, and sometimes when we're lying, we touch our noses.

We even use our bodies to help our listeners understand us when we speak to them:

* Just as we use a rising inflection with our voices when we ask questions, we also raise our heads at the end of a sentence that asks a question. We also raise our hands and our eyes open wider at the end of a question.
* When we make a statement, our voices go down, and at the same time we tend to tilt our heads down.
* When we're speaking and we have to pause, but we intend to go on speaking, we hold the same pitch. In the same situation, we hold our heads still to signal our intent to continue.
* When we're listening to someone speaking and we get to a part with which we strongly disagree, we make a major shifting of our bodies. Knowing this, salesmen, public speakers and many parents have clues as to how their audiences are accepting what they're saying. If you shift your body when your mother or father is telling you something, they'll notice it. They might not be able to tell you why they feel you don't accept what they've said, but they'll think you don't.
* When we're nervous, we blink much more rapidly and more often than we normally do.
* Children suck their thumbs when they're not feeling really secure. Adults signal this feeling by holding their own hands. Dogs yawn. This has nothing to do with what I'm telling you, but it's interesting. Notice the next time when your dog isn't sure what's going on. I bet he yawns.
* When we're under pressure we have a tendency to rock our bodies. The next time you

see a person doing this rocking, count the number of times they rock in a minute. When people are unsure of their positions, they get security from that heart beat-rhythm. It's thought that they seek the security of their mother's heart beat, both before they were born and just after. If you watch, you'll notice that almost all women, even those who are left-handed, carry their babies in their left arms with their children's heads to the left. The side their hearts are on.

SELECTED REFERENCES
for
READING ABOUT BODY LANGUAGE

If you're interested in reading about body language and learning how we communicate our feelings to others by how we move and hold ourselves, you might look in your library for some of these books:

Szasz, S., *The Body Language of Children*. Foreword by Benjamin Spock. Norton, 1978.

Scheflen, A. *Body Language and Social Order*. Englewood Cliffs, N.J. Prentice Hall 1972.

Wainright, G.R., *Body Language*. NTC Pub. Group, 1993.

Buller, D., *Nonverbal Communication*. Greyden Press, 1994.

Cooper, K., *Bodybusiness: The Sender's & Receiver's Guide to Nonverbal Communications*. Total Comm. 1981.

DeVito, J A., *The Nonverbal Communication Workbook*. Waveland Press, 1989.

Gervais, P E., *How to Unlock the Minds of Others*: Total Communication Using Body Language/ Paradigm. Or, 1993.

Gross, R., *You Don't Need Words*., Scholastic Hardcover, 1991.

Hall, E., *The Silent Language*. Greenwood Press, 1980.

Harper, R., *Nonverbal Communication: The State of the Art*. U Ch Press. 1987.

Leathers, D.G., *Successful Nonverbal Communications*. Macmillan, 1991.

Nelson N., *Body Talk*. Thomson Learning, 1993.

Richmond, V.P.& McCroskey, J C., *Nonverbal Behavior in Interpersonal Relationships*. Allyn 1995.

Ardrey, R., *The Territorial Imperative*. Atheneum, 1969.

Cherry, C., *On Human Communication*. Science Editions, Inc., 1961.

Goffman, E., *Behavior in Public Places*. The Free Press, 1969.

The Silent Language. Doubleday and Co., 1959.

Lorenz, K., *On Aggression*. Harcourt Brace, 1966.

Morris, D., *The Meaning of Human Gestures*. Crown Trade Paperbacks, 1994.

THE ONLY SPEECH YOU'RE LIKELY TO HAVE TO GIVE

The only speech courses that I have ever heard about taught the students to speak in front of groups of people. Of course, that's what public speaking is, but very few people ever have to do that kind of speaking. Ministers, lawyers, advertising executives, school administrators, sales managers, and the presidents of clubs and civic organizations are the people who must talk in front of groups. The rest of us, for the most part, talk to one or two people at a time.

The one speech you might have to or want to give in your life will be one we could call a speech requesting action or change. This might be given at a school board meeting, a zoning committee meeting, a political club, a county commission meeting or a church group. The audiences for such speeches are small. Many times fewer than a dozen people. Most people will not do even this kind of speaking.

This exercise will give you preparation for this type of speech.

UNDERSTANDINGS

There are effective ways to present your dissatisfaction with a situation and make a request for a change. You have to find a way that will work, because it's very easy for groups of people—institutions—to listen attentively to people who wish the institutions to change something, and then to ignore their requests. Institutions have a kind of inertia about their activities which makes it much easier for them to continue doing the same things they always have done than to change anything. Groups running institutions have what we call their own agenda. This means that they have goals that are consistent with what the institution wants and not what the institution was created to do for other people.

An example might help. Think of what the public schools were created for. They were established to provide education to young people. That was their only purpose, to train children. Look at what they've become. This may be the reason you're homeschooling now.

Public education costs the American people much more money than any other public activity, maybe even the military. There are huge numbers of administrators for each system in every town. The schools have 12 years to teach young people what they need to know to function in our society, and yet, thirty percent of seniors in high school can't read above the third or fourth grade level. About eighty-five percent can't write an acceptable essay. About forty percent don't know whether the Civil War came before the Revolutionary War or after. Sixty percent can't understand a train or bus schedule, and almost none of them can compute in fractions or use percentage figures.

Even with this understanding of the failure of our educational institutions, the people running those institutions still strongly resist changing anything that is important that doesn't benefit them. This is why, if you're going to be successful asking such an institution to change something in your favor, you'll have to be very organized and sure of just what you want, and you'll have to know how to ask for it.

When you're speaking to a small group, the same principles apply as when you're speaking to one person. Your job will be to make each person in that group feel that you're talking directly to them. This means that you'll have to look into the eyes of each person again and again. Your eyes will have to be constantly moving from person to person. You won't have any reason or chance to look down at notes, across the room, out the window or anywhere but into the eyes of your audience. This is hard to do, but with practice you can manage it.

You will have to do all the other things you've practiced, like smiling, controlling your body, and reinforcing the reactions you get from your audience.

One of the most important jobs you'll have in this effort is to organize the information that you have and the requests that you make. You'll have to keep in mind that the group you're speaking to probably will not want to do as you ask. If this is something they've been wanting to do, they'd have done it. What you want will probably cost them money or effort or political advantage, and these are things that are hard for groups of people to give up.

If you were to organize your presentation using the outline below, it might help you focus your efforts and control the information your audience receives.

Outline for a Speech of Dissatisfaction
and
Proposal for Changes

Name
Address
Thanks for letting you address the group
Nature of the problem you're going to present

I. The present conditions (what it's like now)
    A. The people involved (who it affects)
    B. Costs (what it costs the people involved)
    C. Problems the conditions present (problems other than money)

II. Proposed Solution
  A. Who it would benefit
  B. Why it would be better than present situation
  C. What it would cost
  D. How it would be paid for (taxes, new bond issue, present budget, donations)
  E. What it would take to implement the solution in terms of:
    1. Personnel (who would be involved)
    2. Organization (how would the people involved be directed or controlled)
    3. Laws (that pertain to change or present condition)
    4. Cooperation between groups (who would organize and how they would do it)
    5. Planning (who would do it and with what authority)
    6. Publicity (who by and at what cost)

III. Benefits
  A. Who would benefit from the change and how
  B. Long term savings (in taxes or institutional budgets)
  C. How this solution would solve the present conditions (Each of the present problems have to be solved by the number. This means that you should number the problems when you first present them and then number them again when you show how they would be solved by your suggestions.)

IV. Request that the group vote today to accept your proposal (You'll have to ask them in so many words to accept your proposal. This means that you'll ask them to vote on it that night, or to give you reasons why that vote has to be delayed, or to tell you what has to be done yet before a vote can be taken.)

When you plan your talk to this group, you must keep in mind that they'll want to listen to you and forget your proposal. The easy way for them to do this is to thank you for your excellent suggestions and tell you that they certainly will look carefully at the situation and study what they must do to help solve the problems that you've pointed out to them. They'll then go on to other business. At this point you've failed, and you'll have to come back again and again to request the same change. The only way to avoid this situation is to have done all of the work for them that they'll use as an excuse to put you off. The following example should make this clear.

Suppose that you want to have the director of public safety in your town put a stop light at the corner where children now have to cross a busy street, and where there is now only a yellow blinking light.

The public safety and public works committee will say to you that they'll have to study the problem.

If, in your preparation for your presentation, you have talked to the following people and have their figures, suggestions, and estimates of cost, and approval for the new light, you can shortstop the committee's efforts to stonewall you or put you off with statements that they have to study the proposal.

1. You've talked to the city attorney and he's given you a letter stating that there is no code or legal reason that there can't be a stop light at that corner.
2. You've talked to the city engineer and he's given you a letter stating that the city has the equipment and time to put in the new light by next week. He put in the letter that the wiring is already in place, and that the only changes necessary are to hang the new fixture.
3. The state highway engineer has sent you a letter telling you that the new light will not violate any state laws or plans and that the state is not opposed to the change in any way.
4. The residents who live in the four blocks surrounding that corner have signed a petition to have the light changed.
5. The local merchants who would be affected by the change have given you letters telling you that they favor the change.
6. The area school principal and the superintendent of schools have both given you letters stating that they approve of the change.
7. Three of the local insurance agencies have given you letters telling you that they feel the change would benefit the residents because of the lowered risk of accidents.
8. The police chief has given you a listing of accidents at that corner over the past five years. He states that he feels that a change to a stop light would solve some of that problem.

You can see, that if you were to present this information and these petitions and letters to the group, they'd have a hard time coming up with reasons to put off making a decision on your proposal.

EXERCISES

It would be good for you to practice just one point of your outline at a time. If you can't get your family to play "group" for you, you can arrange chairs around the dining room table like they might be at a meeting and pretend that the people you're talking to are sitting in them.

There's a good chance that you'll be presenting pictures, graphs, charts, signs, tables, statistics or letters to this group. You should understand that when you give material to people to read, that is what they'll do, read it. This means that they won't be listening to you if you're talking while they're reading. So, if you're going to give people material to look at, you should:

1. Tell them about each piece before you give it to them
2. Tell them what to look at and what it means after you give it to them

3. Don't allow them to discuss the material. This doesn't mean that you should tell them not to talk about it, but that you should keep them busy following your directions about what to look at. The following example may help:

You don't talk about the report until after you have a copy of the report in front of everyone. This example should make this clear:

> *I've given you a report from Police Chief Rogers listing the traffic accidents that have occurred in the last four years at the corner of First and Fairfax. Notice that there are two columns of figures. The one on the left is the property damage accidents and the shorter one on the right is the personal injury accidents. Look at the bottom of the page. The figures there are the totals for both types of accidents that we might be able to avoid with the new light. This is why Chief Rogers was so much in favor of this proposal.*

To practice these skills, you should set a table up as a conference table and ask your family to play "committee" for you. You should have papers you've duplicated, one for each member, and hand them out to the committee. You should direct their attention to what you want them to do and read. It's important that you do this, because you'll find that it's much more complicated than it sounds like it might be.

If you have petitions or letters, you should have copies for every member of the group. After you pass the letters out, you should explain what the letters are saying and why that is important for the decision they'll have to make. It might sound similar to this:

> *I'd like you to look at a letter I received from the All State Insurance agency here in town. Here, let me just get one of these to everyone. . . there we are. Now, if you'll read with me the first paragraph where Mr. Brown explains why it's so important that we put up the light.*

> I wish to add my support to your efforts to have a stop light placed at the corner of First and Fairfax. We have processed a large number of claims resulting from accidents at that corner in the past and feel that something must be done.

> *Now, if you'll just pass that letter back to me, I'd like you to look at one from the City Engineer.*

4. Collect each piece after you hand it out or ask them to turn over the piece you've just looked at as you give them a new piece. This will prevent them from looking at the last piece as you talk about the new handout. It might sound similar to this:

> *This first photograph was taken at 3:05 on a school day just two weeks ago. You can see that there are about 15 children standing on the corner*

waiting to cross First Street. You can see that there's no crossing guard.
These children have to wait for a break in traffic to cross. Some of them
appear too young to make safe decisions.

Now, if you'll put that photo aside, I have a chart that I'd like you to
look at. Here let me collect the pictures as I pass these out. There. Now,
if you'll look at the street map of the area around the school, you'll see that
there are stop lights at every busy intersection except the one at First and
Fairfax. That's the one here in the right lower corner, the one circled with
red marker.

5. If you use charts that you hold or put on a stand, make sure that the printing is big enough to be seen clearly by the person in the group who is furthest away. You should test this by putting the sign up and going to the farthest chair and seeing if you can read it clearly.

6. If you're using graphs or charts, you'll have to explain to the group how to read them and also explain the significance of the lines or bars. You should tell your audience what to look at on the chart. If you don't do this, they'll be looking all over the place and you won't get your message across. You might say something similar to this example:

I'd like you to look at this chart on the stand here. I'll have to turn the
cover sheet over. . .there. This is a chart of the traffic flow at the corner of
First and Fairfax. The red bar is the vehicle traffic and the blue bar is
pedestrian traffic. Cars and kids.

The chart is constructed so that the vertical numbers indicate the number
of crossings and the horizontal numbers indicate the times of day of the
crossings of both children and cars. Please notice that both bars are at the
highest point at 7:45 in the morning. This is when the kids are headed to
school and the drivers are headed to work. Both groups are in a hurry.

As you can see, this is a corner waiting for a child to be hit by a car.

It may seem to you that you're holding the hands of your audience too much by directing their attentions so closely. This is necessary. If you don't, they won't understand the chart because they won't take the time to study it. They'll have to be told where and how to look. Practice this with your family. Make a few large charts, and as you hold them up or prop them up, tell them where to look and what to look for. This will take some practice, but it'll be worth it to you.

7. If you have photographs to use as demonstration for a point, you should make slides, if possible, and project them on a screen so all members can see them at once. There is nothing that will break down your presentation faster than to have a group of people all looking at different pictures.

It would be really good practice for you to think about actually giving this speech to a group in your town. Think of how nice it might be if the homeschooled kids in your town could use the public school facilities when they want to. You could then use the pool, playing fields and library. You might be able to learn from your local support leader how to find out which towns now allow homeschoolers to use public facilities. You could contact those support leaders and the school personnel and learn how well it works for them.

You would have to do all of the background work on your presentation, like talking to:

1. The State Department of Education
2. The attorney general for the state
3. The local school's lawyer
4. The principal of the local school
5. The head custodian and the president of the custodian's union
6. The local PTA
7. The teachers' organization
8. The members of your support group who might want to use the facilities, so that you would have an idea of the number of kids who might be involved

You would have to have answers to problems such as:

1. Adult supervision (You should have a list of volunteers.)
2. Insurance
3. Janitor overtime cost
4. Property damage responsibility
5. Equipment wear and damage
6. Who or what group would be responsible (names, address and phone numbers)

You just might be successful, and you'd have a great time!

Order Form

To place your *Writing Strands* order, simply fill out this form and send it to us by mail or by fax. If you would like to get your order started even faster, go to the *Writing Strands* website and place your order online at: www.writingstrands.com

	QTY	Total
Writing Strands 1 Oral Work for ages 3-8 $14.95 ea.	___	_____
Writing Strands 2 About 7 years old $18.95 ea.	___	_____
Writing Strands 3 Starting program ages 8-12 $18.95 ea.	___	_____
Writing Strands 4 Any age after Level 3 or starting program at age 13 or 14 $18.95 ea.	___	_____
Writing Strands 5 Any age after Level 4 or starting program at age 15 or 16 $20.95 ea.	___	_____
Writing Strands 6 17 or any age after Level 5 $20.95 ea.	___	_____
Writing Strands 7 18 or any age after Level 6 $22.95 ea.	___	_____
Writing Exposition Senior high school and after Level 7 $22.95 ea.	___	_____
Creating Fiction Senior high school and after Level 7 $22.95 ea.	___	_____
Evaluating Writing Parents' manual for all levels of *Writing Strands* $19.95 ea.	___	_____
Reading Strands Parents' manual for story and book interpretation, all grades $22.95 ea.	___	_____
Communication and Interpersonal Relationships Communication Manners (teens) $17.95 ea.	___	_____
Basic Starter Set (SAVE $5.00) *Writing Strands 2, Writing Strands 3, Reading Strands* and *Evaluating Writing* $75.80 per set	___	_____
Intermediate Starter Set (SAVE $10.00) *Writing Strands 3, Writing Strands 4, Evaluating Writing, Communication and Interpersonal Relationships* and *Reading Strands* $88.75 per set	___	_____
Advanced Starter Set (SAVE $30.00) *Writing Strands 5, Writing Strands 6, Writing Strands 7, Writing Exposition, Creating Fiction, Evaluating Writing, Communication and Interpersonal Relationships* and *Reading Strands* $138.60 per set	___	_____
Dragonslaying Is for Dreamers – Package 1st novel in *Dragonslaying* trilogy (Early teens) and parents' manual for analyzing the novel. $18.95 ea.	___	_____
Dragonslaying Is for Dreamers Novel only $9.95 ea.	___	_____
Axel Meets the Blue Men 2nd novel in *Dragonslaying* trilogy (Teens) $9.95 ea.	___	_____
Axel's Challenge Final novel in *Dragonslaying* trilogy (Teens) $9.95 ea.	___	_____
Dragonslaying Trilogy All three novels in series $25.00 set	___	_____
Dragonslaying Trilogy and Parents' Manual Three novels plus parents' manual for first novel $32.99 set	___	_____

SUBTOTAL (use this total to calculate shipping) _____

Texas residents: Add 8.25% sales tax _____

U.S. Shipping: $6 for orders up to $75 _____

  $8 for orders over $75

Outside U.S. Shipping: $4 per book. **$12 minimum.** _____

TOTAL U.S. FUNDS

Mail your check or money order or fill in your credit card information below:

○ VISA   ○ Discover   ○ Master Card

Account Number _____

Expiration date: Month _____ Year _____

Signature **X** _____

**We ship UPS to the 48 states, so please no P.O. Box addresses.
PLEASE PRINT**

Name _____

Street _____

City _____ State ____ Zip _____

Phone (_____) _____

Email _____

SHIPPING INFORMATION
CONTINENTAL U.S.: We ship via UPS ground service. Most customers will receive their orders within 10 business days.

ALASKA, HAWAII, U.S. MILITARY ADDRESSES AND US TERRITORIES: We ship via U.S. Priority Mail. Orders generally arrive within 2 weeks.

OUTSIDE U.S.: We generally ship via Air Mail. Delivery times vary.

RETURNS
Our books are guaranteed to please you. If they do not, return them within 30 days and we'll refund the full purchase price.

PRIVACY
We respect your privacy. We will not sell, rent or trade your personal information.

INQUIRIES AND ORDERS
Phone: (800) 688-5375
Fax: (888) 663-7855 TOLL FREE
Write: *Writing Strands*
  624 W. University, Suite 248T
  Denton, TX 76201-1889
E-mail: info@writingstrands.com
Website: www.writingstrands.com

Writing Strands

TO ORDER EVEN FASTER, GO ONLINE AT:

www.writingstrands.com

Prices valid through 01/31/05